Precision

Principles, Practices and Solutions for the Internet of Things

Timothy Chou, PhD

Precision the Movie

Precision "the Movie" with special features is also available for mobile and online, providing the following:

- 29 chapter movie, so you can learn by watching and listening,
- Movie script / book, readable like an eBook,
- Slides images to assist you in teaching IoT to others,
- Exam so you can test yourself on how well you understand the content, and
- Periodically updated, so you can keep up to date as Dr. Timothy Chou continues to update Precision to keep in step with the evolution of the Internet of Things

To receive a complimentary trial version of Precision the movie, please email us at precision@crowdstory.com.

Learn more at http://www.crowdstory.com/precision

Discover more books by Dr. Timothy Chou at http://www.crowdstory.com/timothy-chou

Acclaim for Precision

"The promise of the Internet of Things isn't delivered by connected devices or machines. The promise is in the data that they generate and the insight that can be mined from it. Dr. Chou's IoT Framework presents an excellent roadmap for enterprises struggling to transition the IoT promise to realized value."

— Dr. James Goodnight, CEO, SAS

"A glimpse into how modern technology will affect methods of doing business today, tomorrow and for future generations. This is a must read informative guide for anyone who is truly connected. Read it. Read all of it."

— Martin Richenhagen, Chairman, President and CEO, AGCO

"Our ability to capture and process the data coming from the inter-connectivity of things is critical. Connected devices have increasingly more to tell us. Precision sheds light on the technical and organizational challenges that lay ahead on this next major step in enterprise computing, and shares many real solutions implemented in the world of IoT today."

— Vinod Kumar, CEO, Tata Communications Group

"IoT represents a real opportunity for new enterprise applications. Precision does an excellent job of identifying the key attributes of the technologies that will be required to connect and collect data from Things and turn them into game-changing insights and business models."

— Rob Bearden, CEO, Hortonworks

"Love the framework and the practical approach. It has already helped me identify strengths and gaps in our current IoT strategy."

— Helge Jacobsen, VP Operations Excellency, United Rentals

"I'm devouring this. Scary isn't it? [I] might be becoming a techie."

> — Mark Taylor, Vice President, Global Channel
> Pitney Bowes

"Truly impressive work. Most remarkable is the simple, intuitive and consistent framework. It can be consumed by every audience, plus a rich set of cases, making the whole lofty IoT so close to us and so much more real that it can be touched right there with your fingers. To the CIO/CTOs who are still scratching their heads where to start, this will give them a sense of direction and a sense of urgency."

> — Jane Ren, President, Atomiton, Inc.
> Former Chief Business Architect, General Electric

"Timothy Chou has authored an outstanding compendium of relevant issues and real life applications of Internet of Things. As an ardent aficionado of artificial intelligence, I find this work to be beyond calculable value for understanding the essence of interconnectivity and artificial intelligence."

> — Anthony Chang, MD, MBA, MPH
> Chief Intelligence and Innovation Officer
> Children's Hospital of Orange County

"As an investor and business manager I find Tim Chou's books uniquely informative, clear and timely. Tim identifies important technologies early in their emergence. His clear explanations dispel the fog of jargon and hype. He provides cogent examples of companies implementing IoT to solve genuine business problems and of companies building IoT solutions for profit. His books should be essential reading for any business person touched by technology. Which is everyone."

> — Mick Hellman
> Founder and Managing Partner, HMI Capital, LLC

Precision

*Principles, Practices and
Solutions for the
Internet of Things*

Timothy Chou

CrowdStory Publishing
http://www.crowdstory.com

ISBN 978-1-329-84356-1
Printed in the United States of America
Edition 1.4

Foreword

It is no secret that technology brings change – fast. And it has been proven that the businesses that are able to embrace the change and use it to their advantage are the ones that survive and thrive. In the industrial space we are at a moment where technology is leading business strategy. That means that leaders need to rapidly embrace and understand how technology can and should affect their business. Timothy has had a front seat working with the leaders in the industry who are mastering the realizing of value from the merger of physical and digital.

For many, this merger is uncomfortable because when you start – you don't always know where you will end up. You might end up on a path that leads you to make a change in a business model, a change in how your organization works or a change in how you view your competition. Sometimes it can even change the definition of who you compete with. At GE, we had to make some of these tough decisions as part of our own transformation. It wasn't easy and we didn't do it overnight. One key lesson is that one must always be learning to be successful on a digital journey.

Until now, most industrial business has been focused on making or owning the asset; essentially, everything that goes into designing, building, operating and maintaining an asset. Business leaders could focus on making improvements to things that were familiar or comfortable. Processes could be made leaner. People could be trained in Six Sigma to gain advantage. Now, thanks to technology, everywhere you look it is about how to get the best outcome from that asset. Those same assets can be monitored and operated in entirely new ways – driving improvements like never before. Better speeds, more information, better experience and more productivity – in short, better outcomes from every asset and industrial process. Industrial data coupled with the best analytics are becoming the center of competitive advantage.

The best companies of the future will be those that are able to master the emerging world of connected machines, capture new sources of information from sensors and build deep learning capabilities, all of which helps gain insights and get the most out of physical infrastructure. We are entering a world where we have a greater level of precision to our decision making than ever before. We will drive new levels of productivity that will become the driving force for the world's economy.

Figuring out how to best capitalize on the Industrial Internet can be daunting and confusing. Here in Precision, Dr. Chou is helping to demystify the processes behind getting better outcomes from assets of any kind – machines, real estate, people, factories, etc.; from the initial setup of an organization's IOT framework to defining the principles behind the operations and on to examples and best practices. With a proven case study approach, Timothy has gathered the right examples to help leaders grasp what they need to do and how to do it.

This book is approachable by any business or technical leader. It not only describes the promise, but more importantly makes the process of shifting your thinking and building your own strategy and plan easy to understand.

In the future every business will be a digital business. William Gibson's quote "The future is here – it's just not evenly distributed" is very apropos to the current state of affairs. It is important for businesses to begin their journey to being digital. This book provides both the crystal ball into the future as well as a roadmap to get started.

Bill Ruh
CEO, GE Digital and Chief Digital Officer, GE
April 2016, San Ramon, CA

Contents

Figures

Acknowledgements

While writing a book can sometimes feel like a solo effort, it truly does take a village. This book would not be possible without the insights, knowledge and reviews of countless people, some who will remain nameless due to a desire for anonymity.

I wanted to write a book that would give the reader a useful, conceptual framework to think about this coming generation of enterprise software — one that is practical and not metaphorical. Much of that practical information comes from real cases of what innovative people are doing in the field. I'd particularly like to thank Nick August of August Farms, Leroy Walden at McKenney's, Charles Boicey at Clearsense and Roger Pilc, Robert Mattis and Greg Skinger at Pitney Bowes. I'd also like to acknowledge Kevin Klein, whom I never met but worked with on the Pitney Bowes case. Kevin tragically passed away in a car accident in October 2015. Furthermore, I'd like to thank Greg Hrebek at New York Air Brake; Sebastian Gass and Alysia Green at Chevron (go Stanford!); Biren Gandi and Steve Steinhilber at Cisco; Dan Heintzelman, Nithiyakumar Parameswaran, Christine Englund, Kristi Lundgren, Vivek Shah and Jeremiah Stone at General Electric; Howard Heppelmann and Beth Bambaruch at PTC; Helge Jacobsen at United Rentals, Steve Potmas at Sysmex, Ben Synman at Joy Global; Peter Blackmore, Melissa Runge and Mike Rider at AGCO; Dhrupad Trivedi at Belden; Anthony Sethill, Richard Barnes and Kevin Smith of SensiumVitals; Haranath Varanasi from Tata Consultancy; Kathleen Sico at Duke Power; Brad Klenz at SAS; Jennifer White at SElinc; Pascal Lavoie at IAAH; Melissa Aquino at McCrometer; Wido Menhardt at Beckman; Jesper Frederiksen and Kevin Chance at Danaher Group; Nick Hughes at Lecida; and Bryan Kester and Vlad Yavichev at Autodesk Fusion Connect.

Much of the real detail would not be possible without the help of Jon Leedavey at Vodafone and Stephen Raymond at ERT; Just Sears and Sam Shah with Hortonworks; Ninco DiCosmo of Honeywell, Prith Banerjee at Schneider, Thorsten Mueller with Bosch, Harriet Green at IBM, John Nesi at Rockwell, Ted Angevaare at Shell Oil and Edgar MacBean at Illumina.

And finally, a special thanks to the editors and reviewers: Felipe Winsberg, my Stanford students, David Wright, Emily Tang, Mark Kwon and Sarah Cooper at M2Mi and Jessica Ehlert, Alisabeth Soto and Vince Vasquez at Crowdstory.com.

Writing a book requires a lot of one's time. I'd like to thank my wife, Sue, and my three daughters, Danielle, Alexandra and Caroline, for always supporting me and giving me the time to learn, teach and do many things over the years. And finally, I'd like to thank my parents, David Yuan-Pin and Mary Ann Mei-En Chou, who were both teachers and, whether by genetics or environment, inspired me to try to understand the world well enough to explain it to others.

Preface

I've had many wonderful opportunities in my working life. For instance, I had the opportunity to work for one of the first Kleiner Perkins Caufield & Byers startups, Tandem Computers, developed the cloud computing business at Oracle, and taught at Stanford University for nearly 35 years. About 15 years ago I wrote a book called *The End of Software*, which outlined the fundamental economic reasons that would drive enterprise software to be delivered as a cloud service. In that book, three young companies were called out as great examples, two of which — NetSuite and Salesforce — would later become major public companies.

All of this led me to wonder: what was next for enterprise software? Are we done? Is the business mature? The quick answer is: no. So, what's next?

I've also had the good fortune to work with some large companies like General Electric, who are pioneering what they call the Industrial Internet, and one of the best enterprise accelerators, Alchemist, who has focused its energies on launching young startups in the Internet of Things (IoT) space. This, and my interactions with some insightful Stanford students, led me to realize that for the past 25 years we've been working on Internet of People (IoP) applications; and the next step is going to be applications of the Internet of Things.

Why? Up until now, most business computing has been focused on back-office functions — purchasing, hiring, benefits, accounting. We've built software to automate many of these and while you can debate effectiveness, it's largely a solved problem. These improvements in operational efficiency through CRM or ERP software are good, but hardly transformative. It's really only in the areas of retail (think Amazon) and banking (think eTrade, PayPal) where software has transformed businesses.

In the fundamental infrastructure of the planet — power, water, transportation, healthcare and agriculture — little has changed; but that may no longer need to be the case. With the economics of cloud computing, the vast amount of open-source software and the decreasing cost of sensors, we stand ready to not only digitally transform manufacturers of wind turbines, trucks and trains, but also the industries they equip — healthcare, mining, agriculture. Reaching even farther on a planet with limited resources, as well as allowing machines to operate more precisely, will result in a more precise planet, where we produce and consume energy, water, food and healthcare not as the crude caveman of our roots, but as modern, technology-enabled people.

So why write a book?

Well, the first reason is that I needed to understand the subject and there is no better way than to try to explain it to someone else. I'm still learning, but I think I can help you understand the fundamental building blocks of technology and how these are currently being applied across multiple manufacturers of machines and the industries they serve.

Not Metaphorical

This book is not metaphorical. While I just talked about how this technology might change the planet, our focus is going to be on the practical. We'll try to explain all of the acronyms and use them so you'll be able to talk to others in the field. The audience for this book is business people who need to understand the technology, as well as technology people who need an introduction to the domains of healthcare, agriculture, transportation and energy.

Not Just the Facts

While there will be plenty of specific facts, it's also important to meet some of the characters who are pioneering IoT applications and understand some of their stories. In a fast-moving industry, it's important to understand what some of the other tribes have done.

Not Technology Vendor Centric

This book does not tell the story from one vendor's point of view. We've created a vendor-neutral framework and you'll see how hundreds of companies are contributing.

Not Fragmented

As you will see, IoT applications can be complex and span many domains. Rather than focusing deeply on one particular area (say, connecting Things), this book gives a complete picture.

I wrote this book for students, young and old. I get to teach at Stanford University, but have also delivered guest lectures at MIT, Columbia, Northwestern Rice and UC Berkeley. What I see when I talk to these students is a group of people who are uninterested in building the next social network or dating site, but instead want to put their talents to work for something greater.

As we'll discuss later in more detail, the developing economies of the world — South East Asia, Latin America and Africa — will both fuel global economic development as their populations grow, but also require first-world infrastructure in power, water, healthcare and agriculture. Do you think this will happen the same old way, or will technology play a hand?

Read on.

Book 1: Principles and Practices

1

Introduction – Principles and Practices

Many people think the Internet of Things (IoT) is about your toaster talking to your refrigerator. While there will no doubt one day be very useful consumer IoT applications, the focus of this book is on applications of the enterprise IoT. This book is a practical guide to a complete vendor-agnostic framework for business and technology professionals. Enterprise IoT applications are complex and without a framework; it can be difficult to separate hype from reality. For each of the five layers of the framework — Things, Connect, Collect, Learn, Do — we'll cover a handful of key principles that are important today and in the future. As a practical guide, we also want to make sure you understand how these principles are used in practice today. Finally, we'll put all five layers together and take you through current cases of building precision machines and the impact those might have on modern infrastructure: power, water, agriculture, transportation and healthcare.

Economics

Before we get started it's important to understand that the opportunity to build precision Things and operate them more precisely is being made possible because of fundamental shifts in the economics of computing.

The move of enterprise applications (e.g., financial, sales, marketing, purchasing, payroll, human resource management) to the cloud has been driven by an order of magnitude shift in economics. This is because the true cost of enterprise applications is not the purchase price, but instead the cost to manage the security, availability, performance and change in the application and all of the supporting hardware and software. A simple rule of thumb is that the cost to manage an enterprise application is four times the purchase price per year, which means in four years you'll spend 16 times the purchase price to manage the application. The fundamental cost component to manage the applications is human labor. While finding lower labor rate countries has resulted in some decreases in cost, there is a floor.

Enterprise application cloud services are significantly lower cost because they have standardized their processes and infrastructure, and automated the management of security, availability, performance and change, thereby replacing human labor with computers. This same principle is now being applied to compute and storage infrastructure, resulting in dramatically lower costs and increased flexibility.

I started teaching a class on cloud computing at Tsinghua University in China a few years ago. And to help with the class, the Amazon AWS team was kind enough to donate $3,000 worth of compute time. At the time, that would buy a small server in Northern Virginia for 3.5 years, which interestingly didn't get any of the

4

students excited. On the other hand, $3,000 would also buy 10,000 computers for 30 minutes, which got everybody thinking.

Not Internet of People

Most first and second-generation enterprise software was focused on us — people, individuals or groups. People in the enterprise software space had to do this because these applications had to do something useful, like help us buy a book, issue a purchase order, recruit more employees or communicate with others.

But Things aren't people. This may seem obvious, but let's discuss three fundamental differences.

A Lot More Things Than People

These days, you can't be on the Internet and not see some pronouncement about how many Things are going to become connected. John Chambers, former CEO of Cisco, recently declared there will be 500 billion Things connected by 2024. That's nearly 100x the number of people on the planet.

Things Can Tell You More Than People

The main mechanism people use to tell applications something is a keyboard, and most applications use some kind of form to collect simple amounts of data from each of us. Things have many more sensors. A typical cell phone has nearly 14 sensors, including an accelerometer, GPS and even a radiation detector. Industrial Things like wind turbines, gene sequencers or high-speed inserters can easily have 100 sensors.

Things Can Talk Constantly

Most of the data from the Internet of People (IoP) applications comes from either encouraging us to buy something or making it part of the hiring process. In short, people don't enter data frequently into an ecommerce, human resources (HR), purchasing, customer relationship management (CRM) or enterprise resource planning (ERP) application. On the other hand, a utility grid power sensor can send data 60 times per second, a construction forklift once per minute, and a high-speed inserter once every two seconds.

Things aren't people.

Next Generation Enterprise Software

The first generation of enterprise application software from SAP, Oracle, Siebel, PeopleSoft and Microsoft leveraged the availability of low-cost, client-server computing to automate key financial, HR, supply chain and purchasing processes. The business model was based on licensing the application software with the purchasing company left with the responsibility (and cost) of managing the security, availability, performance and change in the software.

In 2000, the second generation of enterprise application software began. It was largely differentiated by a fundamental shift in the delivery model. In the second generation, the software provider took on the responsibility of managing the software; and with that change also came a change to the business model. Rather than an upfront licensing fee, a software-as-a-service (SaaS) model emerged, which allowed customers to purchase the service monthly or annually. You've probably heard of many suppliers from this era including Salesforce.com, WebEx, Taleo, SuccessFactors, NetSuite, Vocus, Constant Contact and Workday, to name a few.

As a result, most of the basic function — sales, marketing, purchasing, hiring, benefits, accounting — have been automated. While you can debate effectiveness, it's largely a solved problem; however, these improvements in operational efficiency through CRM or ERP software are good, but hardly transformative. It's really only in the areas of retail (think Amazon) and banking (think eTrade, PayPal) that software has transformed businesses.

Perhaps now, with the changing economics of computing, the continued innovations in communications technology and decreasing cost of sensors, we can move to the third generation of enterprise software and tackle the challenges of precision agriculture, power, water, healthcare and transportation, and fundamentally reshape businesses and our environment.

Internet of Things

IoT has somewhat become like the old story of the blind men and the elephant, where each man touches a different, single part of the elephant and therefore have different versions of what the elephant *is*. Meaning, many people have many differing ideas of what IoT *is* exactly. In this book, we're going to establish a framework (with examples) that covers all of the major components of IoT applications. It's a five-layer, vendor-neutral framework that can be used by both technical and business people.

Given this framework, the first book is composed of chapter pairs — principles and practices — for each layer. The principle chapters are meant to describe fundamental technology principles. If you're an expert in machine learning or networking, these chapters will seem trivial. They are instead meant to give the reader an introduction to a handful of fundamental principles that are the foundation of technical products, which are particularly relevant to the IoT. Each of the five principal chapters is paired with a chapter on practices. In these chapters you'll see specific use cases in energy, agriculture, healthcare and transportation, all of which will illustrate some of the fundamental principals in practice.

The second book highlights a series of case studies; there are cases for both manufacturers and users of Things. For example, we have a case on AGCO, a manufacturer of agricultural machines, as well as a case on Nick August, a farmer who uses agricultural machines. By using precision technologies, manufacturers of gene sequencers, wind turbines and forklifts can build precision machines, which will allow them to deliver better service at a lower cost and ultimately, in some cases, fundamentally transform their business models. For those who use these new precision machines including utilities, airlines, hospitals and farms, they will be able to reduce their operating costs, increase the quality of their service, and in many cases, increase the health and safety of their products. In a world that is increasing its population and trying to increase the standard of living, operating a more precise planet will be better for everyone.

Let's get started on the journey.

2

IOT Framework

Whether you're building, buying, selling or investing in technology to enable enterprise IoT applications, it's important to develop a framework you can use to understand the various components or parts of the industry. Furthermore, business and technology people should understand the framework. And finally, while there are players who would like to provide many parts of the solution, it's valuable to have a vendor-independent framework.

In this chapter we'll focus on defining the various parts of an IoT framework, which is composed of five major layers: Things, Connect, Collect, Learn and Do. We'll then take a few of the companies that are providing several (but not all) of the components and map them to the framework. Of course, these will not be the only products we'll highlight in this book.

IoT Framework

Figure 2.1 IoT Framework

The first layer is composed of Things. We'll use the words *Thing*, *machine* and *equipment* interchangeably in this book. Things focus on the machines themselves and are connected to the Internet in many different ways. Once connected, Collect refers to the technologies designed to collect the data, which are increasingly time-series data being sent every hour, minute or second. The fourth layer is Learn. Unlike in the world of IoP applications where we had to entice you to type something, IoT applications will get data constantly. For the first time, we can use machines to learn from our Things at the hospital, mine or farm, for example. Finally, you should ask, what's all this technology for? What are the business outcomes? The Do layer describes both the software application technologies and the business models affected by companies that build Things, as well as those who use them to deliver healthcare, transportation or construction services, for example.

Things

Enterprise Things, whether that's a gene sequencer, locomotive or water chiller, are becoming smarter and more connected. If you're going to build or buy the next-generation machines, you'll need to consider sensors, CPU architectures, operating systems, packaging and security. Sensors are beginning to follow Moore's Law and becoming dramatically lower in cost every year. These sensors are increasingly attached to low-cost computers, which can range from simple microcontrollers to fully featured CPUs supporting either the ARM or Intel instruction set architecture. As you move to more powerful processors, more powerful software can be supported, and that software becomes the point of vulnerability in an increasingly hostile world.

Connect

Things can be connected to the Internet in a variety of ways. Connecting Things requires a diverse set of technologies based on the amount of data that needs to be transmitted, how far it needs to go, and how much power you have. Furthermore, you have many choices at a higher level on how to manage the connection and how it's protected and secured.

Collect

Things aren't people. The sheer volume of data that can be generated by Things will be exponentially larger than that of IoP applications. Data might be collected and stored using SQL, NoSQL, traditional time-series and next-generation, time-series collection architectures.

Learn

With an increasing amount of data coming from Things, we'll need to apply technology to learn from that data. Learning and analysis products will include query technology and both supervised and unsupervised machine-learning technologies. Because, as an industry, we have mostly focused on IoP applications, most of the technology applied to learning from data streams has been applied to learning from data about people. As with all parts of the stack, there is room for future innovation.

Do

As it was with IoP applications, there will be both packaged applications (e.g., ERP, CRM) and middleware to build IoT applications. Of course in the end, these applications — whether bought or built — have to drive business outcomes. As machines become increasingly complex and enabled by software, many of the lessons learned in software maintenance and service will also apply to a machine service. As many in the software industry already know, the movement to delivering software as a service has revolutionized the industry.

To attach the framework to real products, we'll use five suppliers who provide many (but not all) of the components of the IoT framework. Our objective here is to illustrate some of the similarities and differences.

Build Machines

When General Electric (GE) Vice Chairman, Daniel Heintzelman, delivered a guest lecture to my Stanford class, he discussed the impact that former GE chairman and CEO, Jack Welch, had on the company. What you may not know is how Welch was integral in moving GE from being just a provider of machines (like jet engines), to providing service contracts on those machines. The result of that focus is that GE sold service contracts valued at nearly $50 billion in 2014. Furthermore, they ended 2014 with about $189 billion in multi-year service agreements.

Current GE CEO, Jeff Immelt — realizing that service is powered by software and information — took another big step in 2011 and hired William (Bill) Ruh to lead a significant investment into software. Headquartered in San Ramon, CA, this software group has developed Predix, a platform for building industrial IoT applications.

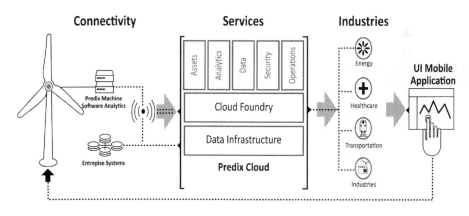

Figure 2.2 GE IoT Framework

Unlike a traditional software company, GE builds machines. As an example, GE's new gas turbine weighs over 400 tons, has 3,000 sensors and generates enough electricity to power 400,000 homes.

But now, GE also builds software. For instance, Predix Machine is their device-independent software stack to **connect** machines to the Internet; it brings data from various sensors and devices into the Predix Cloud. Data is **collect**ed in the Predix Data Services, which provides time-series service, as well as an enterprise SQL-on-Hadoop analytic engine. **Learn**ing is implemented by Predix Analytics Services, which provide a framework for developing and embedding advanced analyses in business operations. Some middleware services such as Predix Security Services and a UI builder are also made available. Finally, one of the things you can **do** with the data is asset, thing and machine modeling; the Predix Asset service enables application developers to create and store assets. For example, a developer can create an asset model that describes the logical component structure of all pumps in an organization, and then create instances of that model to represent each pump.

There are a group of companies like GE (e.g., Bosch and Schneider Electric) that also build Things and are taking steps to power machines with software and provide their software to others.

Not Machine Builder

PTC is an example of a company that does not build machines. PTC has built a one billion dollar business in two major areas: Computer Aided Design and Product Lifecycle Management. With almost 250,000 CAD-application subscribers and 1.6 million PLM-application subscribers, the revenues are almost evenly split. To fuel growth, PTC has focused heavily on IoT software; and given their existing customer base they have a distinct advantage in the ability to bring products to the market. Recently, their CFO said they are targeting over $50 million in sales, but more importantly, 40% growth. Sterling Auty of JP Morgan Chase says, "The subscription transition trend reemerged, and in fact our favorite stock for 2016 is PTC, a name that is undergoing a transition, but will also benefit from the fast growth secular trend in IoT."

In Harvard Business Review's November 2014 article, "How Smart, Connected Products Are Transforming Competition," Harvard professor and PTC board member, Michael Porter and PTC CEO, Jim Heppelman, discussed PTC's vision and the ten new strategic choices facing companies in this new competitive landscape. They conclude by writing:

> *Smart, connected products are changing how value is created for the customers, how companies compete, and the boundaries of competition itself. These shifts will affect virtually every industry, directly or indirectly/ But smart, connected products will have a broader impact than this. They will affect the trajectory of the overall economy, giving rise to the next era of IT-driven productivity growth for companies, their customers, and the global economy.*

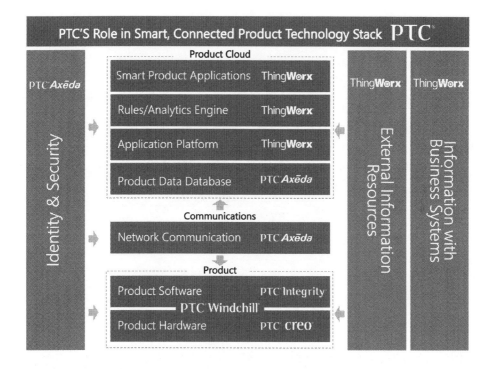

Figure 2.3 PTC IoT Framework

PTC doesn't manufacture **Things**; however, Windchill, a product lifecycle management application and Creo, a CAD application, can be used to build next-generation machines. PTC's Axeda provides cloud-based service and software for **connect**ing products and machines. Axeda also provides **collect**ion services. ColdLight, another acquisition, is the basis of their **learn**ing technology. ColdLight's Neuron analyzes data, detects patterns, builds statistically validated predictive models, and sends information to virtually any type of application or technology. Finally, the middleware to help build applications to **do** something with the data comes from ThingWorx. ThingWorx has been used to implement predictive maintenance and system-monitoring apps, which PTC says enables significantly faster deployment of applications than conventional technology.

Industry

Figure 2.4 IoT Industry Examples

While GE and PTC represent two large companies making significant investments in software, the industry is considerably larger. Later, we'll discuss other suppliers of Things, technology to build Things and solutions for connecting Things, collecting the data, learning from it, and doing something with it. As with any emerging area, like cloud computing, there are both established players and startups. We will not discuss all of them, but hopefully you'll get a sense of who some of the current players are and the potential for the future. Figure 2.3 shows some of the players that are discussed later.

Summary

For the remainder of this book, we'll use the Things, Connect, Collect, Learn and Do framework. First, we'll dive into each of the components and discuss fundamental principles and show you how these principles are put into practice. At the end, we'll discuss complete solutions implemented by both manufacturers of precision machines, as well as those who use them to implement precision agriculture, power, water, healthcare or transportation.

3

Things Principles

Enterprise Things — whether that's a gene sequencer, locomotive, or water chiller — are becoming both smarter and more connected. In this chapter, we'll cover some of the fundamental principles you should be aware of when building the next enterprise Thing. Sensors are beginning to follow Moore's Law and becoming dramatically less expensive each year. These sensors are becoming increasingly attached to low-cost computers, which can range from simple microcontrollers to fully featured CPUs supporting either the ARM or Intel instruction set architecture. As you move to more powerful processors, more powerful software can be supported, so we'll cover some basic operating systems. Finally, we'll discuss a couple security fundamentals that anyone building enterprise Things needs to consider.

Sensors

While there are hundreds of kinds of sensors, we're going to use your phone to get more specific. Let's start with one of the most commonly used sensors: the accelerometer. As its name implies, it measures the acceleration the handset is experiencing relative to free fall. The same sensor is also used to determine a device's orientation along its three axes. Apps use this data to tell if a phone is in portrait or landscape orientation and if its screen is facing upward or downward. The gyroscope is another sensor that can provide orientation information but with greater precision. This particular sensor tells you how much a phone has been rotated and in which direction.

Another sensor is the magnetometer. The magnetometer measures the strength and the direction of the magnetic field; it's used both in compass apps and apps made for metal detection.

The proximity sensor works by shining a beam of infrared light that is reflected from the object and picked up by the detector; it is then placed near the earpiece of a phone to let it know you're probably in a call and that the screen has to be turned off.

Phones also have light sensors to measure the brightness of the ambient light; the phone uses this data to automatically adjust the display's brightness.

Some phones have a built-in barometer, which measures atmospheric pressure. It's used to determine its height above sea level, which results in improved GPS accuracy. Every phone has a thermometer and some have more than one. If a component is detected to be overheating, the system shuts itself down to prevent damage. Galaxy pioneered the use of an air-humidity sensor in its phones; data provided by this was used in an app to tell whether or not the user was in his or her "comfort zone" — one with optimal air temperature and humidity.

A pedometer is a sensor used to count the number of steps the user has taken; some phones just use data from the accelerometer, but a dedicated pedometer is more accurate and power efficient. The Google Nexus 5 is among the few phones that have a true pedometer built in. Some phones, such as the Galaxy X5, have heart-rate monitors. This is implemented by detecting the minute pulsations of the blood vessels inside your finger. Of course, most Apple users know about fingerprint sensors as a substitute for a lock screen password.

Finally, a sensor that you wouldn't expect to find is a radiation sensor. The Sharp Pantone 5 features an app to measure the current radiation level in the area. Adding the microphone and the cameras to the list gives us a figure of at least 14 different sensors on just your phone. This is just a small number of all of the potential sensors, as we'll see in subsequent chapters.

Computer Architecture

All smart connected machines contain some kind of central processing unit (CPU) capable of running some software. As Things can be constrained by power consumption, physical size and cost, there are a number of tradeoffs that can be made in the basic architecture of the CPU.

At the most basic level, there are classes of microcontrollers that have simple instruction sets with more limited access to memory storage and generally lower power consumption. An example would be the Arduino, which employs an 8-bit, ATmega series microcontroller manufactured by Amtel. While smaller, cheaper and less functional Things can use microcontrollers; the next step is a fully featured instruction set — at this point either from ARM or Intel.

ARM is a Reduced Instruction Set Computer (RISC), which requires significantly fewer transistors to implement the instruction set than typical Intel x86 processors in most personal computers. As a result, this approach reduces costs, heat and power use. Raspberry Pi is based around a 32-bit ARM processor. The Apple A7, which powers this generation of phones and tablets, is a 64-bit system ARM CPU designed by Apple.

While ARM is in use by many, Intel's x86 architecture still powers lots of servers and laptops and as a result, has many software development tools. Intel Atom is the brand name for a line of ultra-low-power microprocessors from Intel.

Software

There are many different operating system or run-time environments for executing software on a particular Thing. Decisions here will revolve around the memory footprint the software requires, the development environment and the real-time requirements.

Footprint
In computing, the memory footprint of an executable program indicates its runtime memory requirements while the program executes. Larger programs have larger memory footprints. Software programs themselves often do not contribute the largest portions to their own memory footprints; rather, structures introduced by the run-time environment can increase the footprint. In a Java program, the memory footprint is predominantly made up of the Java Virtual Machine (JVM) run-time environment.

Software Development Environment

A software development environment, sometimes called an integrated development environment (IDE), is software that provides comprehensive facilities to computer programmers for software development. A software development environment normally consists of a source-code editor, build automation tools and a debugger. For programming the microcontrollers, the Arduino platform provides an IDE, which includes support for the C, C++ and Java programming languages. As a builder of enterprise Things, you'll have to consider what kind of IDE you'll want for your programmers.

Operating System

An operating system, or run-time environment, contains software that is commonly used by many applications. You're likely familiar with Linux and Microsoft Windows in the world of IoP applications. In IoT applications, there can be the need for what is called real-time operating systems.

A real-time operating system (RTOS) is an operating system intended to serve time-critical applications. Processing time requirements (including any OS delay) are measured in tenths of seconds or shorter. A key characteristic of an RTOS is the level of its consistency concerning the amount of time it takes to accept and complete an application's task. Key factors in a real-time OS are minimal interrupt latency and minimal thread-switching latency; a real-time OS is valued more for how quickly or how predictably it can respond, rather than for the amount of work it can perform in a given period of time. Wind River is an example company that provides a RTOS commonly used to support the needs for real-time processing. Of course, as processors become faster and the needs of any smart machine become wider, we may end up using conventional operating systems in many cases.

Security

There are many aspects of security relevant in the discussion of IoT. For this chapter we're going to focus on the security and integrity of the software. After all, many more security breaches have happened by compromising the software than any other area.

Secure Boot

Whenever the machine powers up, the first software to run is termed "the boot." Secure boot secures the overall booting process by preventing the loading of any software that is not signed with an acceptable digital signature. When secure boot is enabled, it allows a key to be written to the firmware; once the key is written, secure boot allows only software with the key to be loaded.

No Bad Software

Many of you are familiar with antivirus software on your laptops or PCs. Antivirus software is built to detect bad software that could compromise a computer. A very famous case was the Stuxnet virus, which ended up taking over the centrifuges of Iran's uranium enrichment plants. Stuxnet specifically targets programmable logic controllers (PLCs), which are used to control machines — in this case centrifuges — for separating nuclear material. Stuxnet functions by targeting machines using Microsoft Windows OS and networks, and then seeking out Siemens Step 7 software. Stuxnet reportedly ruined almost one-fifth of Iran's nuclear centrifuges.

All Good Software

A patch is a piece of software designed to update a computer's software. While some patches are designed to improve usability or performance, there are also patches designed to repair security vulnerabilities. Patch management is the process of strategizing and planning which patches should be applied to which systems at a specified time. In IoP applications, companies like VMware, Oracle and Microsoft easily release hundreds of relevant security patches per year.

Packaging

Packaging is a major discipline within the field of electronic engineering and it includes a wide variety of technologies. Packaging must consider protection from mechanical damage, cooling, radio frequency noise emission and electrostatic discharge. Industrial equipment made in small quantities may use standardized, commercially available enclosures such as card cages or prefabricated boxes. Mass-market consumer devices may have highly specialized packaging to increase consumer appeal.

One of the packaging technologies used in high volume is called system-on-a-chip (SoC). A SoC is an integrated circuit that combines all components of a computer or other electronic system into a single semiconductor chip. It may contain digital, analog, mixed-signal and often radio-frequency functions. The contrast with a microcontroller is one of degree; microcontrollers typically have fewer than 100KB of memory, whereas a SoC is used for more powerful processors capable of running software that needs a larger memory footprint (e.g., Linux). When it's not feasible to construct a SoC for a particular application, an alternative is a system-in-package (SiP) comprising a number of chips in a single package. In large volumes, a SoC is believed to be more cost effective than a SiP because it increases the yield of the fabrication and its packaging is simpler.

In the next chapter, we'll see a few current examples of enterprise Things.

4

Things in Practice

Today, modern phones can have 14 sensors and you can buy a powerful computer for $100. These two points help to explain why enterprise Things are getting smarter. In this chapter, we'll cover a few examples of the range of machines, as well as the many different ways that they are being made smarter.

Wind Turbines

Next-generation power grids will include renewable power generation. A large wind turbine is capable of generating six megawatts, can cost up to $2.8 million, and weighs in at 450 tons with rotors weighing 55 tons, making them no small machines. So maybe you're not surprised that in each of these wind turbines there can be an HP Intel server with an EMC VNXe storage system. Companies like Vestas can have more than 50,000 wind turbines in the field with

Senvion managing more than 6,000. Amazingly, a very high percentage of these wind turbines are connected.

A wind turbine can have up to 400 sensors. These sensors can deliver information such as wind speed and direction, blade-rotation speed, power generated, component temperature, vibration, noise levels and more. While data can be sampled once every couple of seconds, it's typically packaged and shipped into the cloud once every ten minutes over a VPN-protected network running on DSL or ISDN.

All functions are controlled using the embedded Intel server. The system runs Windows CE, which collects and processes all the data, checks the feed-in and communicates with the cloud. Safety and measurement technology and condition monitoring are part of the software on the wind turbine itself.

Agricultural Machines

Growing grain is an important part of feeding the people on our planet. Farmers use a number of specialized machines; a seed drill makes a small burrow and then deposits the seeds at equal distances and a specific depth; the seeds also get covered with soil, ensuring good germination and saves them from being eaten by birds. The crop also needs fertilizer and this can be done using a broadcast spreader. The basic operating concept of this machine is simple; a large hopper is positioned over a horizontal spinning disk with a series of fins that throw the fertilizer from the hopper out and away from the spreader. Finally, you need to harvest the crop. A combine harvester is a machine that harvests grain crops. The name comes from the combining of three separate operations — reaping, threshing, and winnowing — into a single process. Reaping is the cutting of the grain stalks; threshing is separating the grain from the stalks, which was once done by hitting them with a flail; and winnowing is when the wheat is tossed into the air to separate it from the chaff.

Increasingly, all this equipment is outfitted with sensors. This can be machine data like oil pressure, header height or rotor speed, as well as agronomic data like moisture content or nitrogen level. AGCO globally manufactures many different kinds of equipment and has engineered a hardware module that can be attached to any machine. The AGCO Connectivity Module (ACM) is developed and manufactured as part of a joint venture between AGCO and Appareo called Intelligent Agricultural Solutions (IAS). The module supplies sensor interfaces as well as 2G, 3G, and satellite communications interfaces. In time, ACM will also become a default hardware option for all new AGCO machines. ACM is combined with cloud-based software to provide subscription services for the farmers and the dealers. As an example, when preparing for the coming season, a dealer technician can help farmers get their machines set up for the type of operation they will use it for first. This will ensure that when it's time to go to the field, the machine is ready with only minor adjustments needed. In addition, there are services to ensure the machine is set up to accurately record the agronomic data.

Clinical Hematology Analyzers

Hematology analyzers are used widely in patient and research settings to count and characterize blood cells for disease detection and monitoring. Basic analyzers return a complete blood count (CBC) with a three-part differential white blood cell (WBC) count. Sophisticated analyzers measure cell structure and can detect small cell populations to diagnose rare blood conditions.

The three main physical technologies used in hematology analyzers are: electrical impedance, flow cytometry and fluorescent-flow cytometry. These are used in combination with chemical reagents that alter blood cells to extend the measurable parameters.

The traditional method for counting cells is electrical impedance. It is used in almost every hematology analyzer. Whole blood is passed between two electrodes through an aperture so narrow that only one cell can pass through at a time. The impedance changes as a cell passes through. The change in impedance is proportional to cell volume, resulting in a cell count and measure of volume.

Laser-flow cytometry is more expensive than impedance analysis, due to the requirement for expensive reagents, but returns detailed information about the structure of blood cells. Scattered light is measured at multiple angles to determine the cell's granularity, diameter and inner complexity. These are the same cell characteristics that can be determined by human observation of a slide. Adding fluorescent reagents extends the use of flow cytometry to measure specific cell populations. Fluorescent dyes reveal the nucleus-plasma ratio of each stained cell. Of course the use of these reagents increases the cost of any analysis.

There are a variety of machines from multiple suppliers. Some are used by large-scale clinics. The Sysmex XE-5000 reports 31 whole blood parameters at a rate of 150 samples per hour, while its low end pocH-100 does 25 samples per day. Some analyzers, like the Beckman Coulter LH 780, are capable of reading barcode labels and others can store a large number of results on the analyzer. A small benchtop analyzer can save 1,000 patient results with histograms. The Horiba ABX Pentra DX120 SPS will store 90,000 results plus graphics.

High Volume Mail Inserters

If you send a lot of physical mail, such as a large bank sending out monthly account statements, you'll need to insert the statements into envelopes. Pitney Bowes builds a high-volume inserter called the Epic Inserter, which can stuff envelopes at the rate of 22,000 per hour, while also allowing quick changeovers to different format types.

The inserters are controlled by dozens of servomotors and have hundreds of sensors to monitor the flow of mail and provide feedback to the control system. Specifically, some of these sensors provide information on motor RPM, motor shaft position, velocity of mail material (sheets, envelopes, mail pieces), position and skew of mail material, material thickness and weight, air pressure, and vacuum levels where air is used to control the machine.

The sensors are all attached to local compute and storage, which are one or more industrial PCs mounted inside the machine and networked together to share data and synchronize control of the machine. Current PCs are Intel processors with 4GB of memory and a 500-GB hard drive packaged for a 19-inch rack. The computer is running Microsoft Windows 7 with RTX from IntervalZero, providing real-time extensions for motion control. For security, they use TrendMicro antivirus software.

Locomotives

New York Air Brake (NYAB) has been a leading supplier to the railroad industry for 125 years doing braking systems and components, training simulators and train control systems. NYAB's system, LEADER, is integrated with the locomotive's on-board electronics to provide locomotive engineers with real-time information and coaching via an in-cab display.

NYAB deploys on three hardware platforms. For the U.S. Class 1 market, they use equipment provided by Wabtec, which uses 500MHz Intel processors with 256M of memory, has 512MB of solid-state storage and runs the QNX operating system. QNX is a subsidiary of Blackberry. The second platform is for EMD locomotives. In this case, NYAB software runs on a computer made by Deuta-Werke and interacts directly with the locomotive systems to leverage existing sensors rather than adding their own. Dueta-Werke hardware and software platform is nearly identical to Wabtec.

The final configuration, Quad C, is used for international and U.S. short-line railroads. The Quad C is NYAB's packaging of the National Instruments CompactRIO with a QNX system. In this case, NYAB provides all the sensors and does all the data aggregation. The CompactRIO system runs on a Xilinx Zynq ARM architecture, packaged as a SoC. It runs a special, real-time Linux OS developed by National Instruments. One of the big challenges National Instruments faces in creating platforms for enterprise IoT is getting advanced chipsets to run at higher temperatures without fan cooling. And given the length of time some of these trains are in service, the parts must be made available for ten or more years.

The types of sensor data available includes brake cylinder PSI (the amount of pressure applied to the locomotive's brake cylinders), brake-pipe PSI (the current PSI of the locomotive's brake pipe), equalizing-reservoir PSI (a small reservoir used on locomotives to regulate the brake pipe), brake pipe air flow (a flow meter provides air mass flow rate into the brake pipe), current and voltage to traction motors, speed, engine RPMs and location.

Sensors will typically record data once per second, although some data is sampled at five times per second. NYAB has more than 4,000 of its systems deployed in the field.

Construction Equipment

Construction equipment can include generators, welding machines, scissor lifts, boom lifts and light poles. These machines are increasingly instrumented and SAE J1939 is the standard used for communication and diagnostics. Originating in the U.S. car and heavy-duty truck industry, SAE J1939 is now widely used in other parts of the world. Here are a few examples of the types of data available from a generator:

- Amps Phase A (ST_AMPS_A)
- Cellular Signal Percentage (CELL_SIGNAL)
- Engine Coolant Temperature - Coolant Temperature (ST_COTE)
- Engine Oil Pressure – Oil Pressure (ST_OIL_PR)
- Fuel Level (FUEL_LEVEL)
- Last Communication (COMM_TIME)
- Last Data Collection Time (LAST_DATA)
- Low Coolant Temperature (AL_COTE_LOLO)
- Total KW (ST_KW)
- Voltage Phase A-B (ST_VOLT_A)

While many original equipment manufacturers (OEMs) are starting to provide their own sensors and local computing, some construction rental companies are standardizing on their own designs rather than deal with the heterogeneous nature of using manufacturers' solutions. If you have 3,000 different types of machines, this makes a lot of sense.

Companies like Calamp provide products such as the LMU-5000 as a core component for standardizing across many different types of Things. The LMU-5000 uses a 32-bit 400Mhz ARM processor with 128MB of flash storage; furthermore, it runs a Linux operating system and provides higher level services like TCP/IP, HTTP and VPN. And all of this has to be packaged for a construction environment with temperature, humidity, shock and vibration challenges.

Next

Our devices and machines — our Things — are set to become much smarter. Today for less than $100 you can equip a 1GHz ARM architecture processor with 512MB of memory and 2GB of flash memory storage; the computer is slightly larger than a couple of coins. Furthermore, you'll have Wi-Fi and Bluetooth connectivity and support for a full Linux distribution included. This computer can connect to 128 sensors, which brings us to the rapid decrease in the cost of sensors. Sensors that cost ten dollars today are headed toward costing one dollar. An accelerometer today is less than three dollars. Of course, the last time we ended up with millions of smart Things it was called a PC and Intel dominated on the hardware side and Microsoft dominated on the software side. Will it be the same this time around?

One thing that does not need to be the same is our approach to securing these Things. It's always been a catch-up game, as most of the Things we built for people didn't predict the danger of connecting to global networks. Perhaps this time around, we'll engineer our machines to be able to protect themselves.

5

Connect Principles

Connecting Things requires a diverse set of technologies based on the amount of data that needs to be transmitted, how far it needs to go, and how much power you have. Furthermore, you have many choices at a higher level on how to manage, protect and secure the connection. In this chapter, we'll give you a brief tutorial on connecting machines and some of the fundamental principles. If you work in networking, just skip ahead.

Networking Fundamentals

In networking you'll eventually hear about the OSI stack. The Open Systems Interconnection (OSI) stack is a conceptual model that characterizes and standardizes the communication functions of a telecommunication or computing system, without regard to their underlying internal structure and technology. Its goal is the interoperability of diverse communication systems with standard protocols. The model partitions a communication system into abstraction layers; the original version of the model defined seven layers.

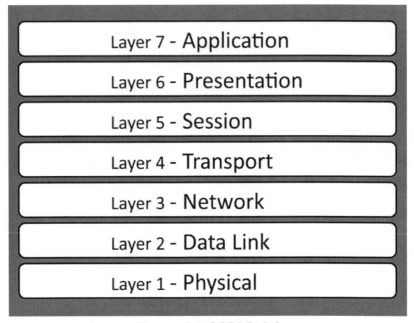

Figure 5.1 OSI Model

A layer serves the layer above it and is served by the layer below it. For example, a layer that provides error-free communications across a network provides the path needed by applications above it, while it calls the next lower layer to send and receive packets that comprise the contents of that path. This stack is a useful framework to understand the different levels of connectivity from a purely electric level all the way to the application level. In this chapter we'll focus on the data-link layer and the higher-level application layer.

Data-link Layer

The data-link layer provides node-to-node data transfer, which is a link between two directly connected nodes. It detects and possibly corrects errors that may occur in the physical layer. It defines the protocol to establish and terminate a connection between two physically connected devices and defines the protocol for flow control between them. The data-link layer is responsible for controlling how devices in a network gain access to data and permission to transmit it. It is also responsible for identifying and encapsulating network layer protocols and controls error checking and packet synchronization. Connection technology including Ethernet, WiFi and ZigBee all operate at the data-link layer.

Range versus Power

While there are cases where one can physically connect the Things to the Internet, either because of location or the fact that the Thing is mobile, you will need some form of wireless technology. There are numerous choices: WiFi, 3G, 4G, ZigBee, NFC, LoRaWan, Satellite, etcetera. Which strategy or strategies you choose depends on a couple of fundamental principles related to power consumption, range requirements, data rates, costs, size of antenna and the environment.

	WiFi	ZigBee	Bluetooth	NFC
POWER	High	Low	Classic: Mid LE/Smart: Low	Tag: Zero Reader: Very Low
RANGE	←————→ 30-100 m	←——→ 10-20 m	↔ 10 m	• <0.1 m

Figure 5.2 Range versus Power

Figure 5.2 shows the tradeoff between range and power consumption for four different connection technologies. WiFi, which has a range of 30-100 meters, requires considerably more power than Bluetooth, which has a maximum range of 10 meters, or NFC, where the range is less than 0.1 meters. Many of you know to turn off WiFi if you want to conserve battery power on your phone.

As a rule, a wireless signal attenuates with the square of distance. Put another way, if you want to double your range, it requires a four-fold increase in power — a bigger battery.

Some applications may be able to operate within a closed, proprietary wireless network. As an example, McCrometer water sensors use the band from 560-480Mhz, which has been allocated for this type of communication. A farm or water district can purchase a license for a portion of this spectrum from the FCC that's good for 10 years and covers a 20-mile radius. At this frequency, UHF is capable of reaching between one and 12 miles, depending on the terrain.

Range versus Data Rate

Another tradeoff is range versus speed. As frequency rises, available bandwidth typically rises, but distance and ability to overcome obstacles is reduced. For any given distance, a 2.4GHz installation will have roughly 8.5dB of additional path loss (3dB is a 50% loss) when compared to 900MHz.

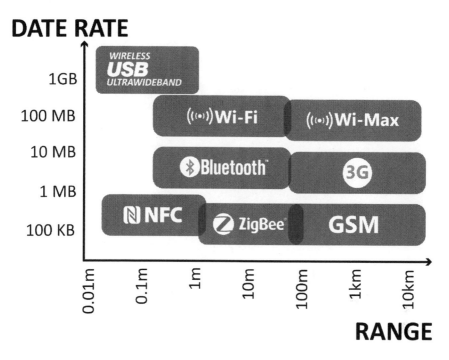

Figure 5.3 Range vs. Data Rate

So, higher frequencies have higher bandwidth capability, but require more power to achieve the same range. Lower frequencies have lower bandwidth, but can achieve longer distance; however, lower frequencies unfortunately require larger antennas to achieve the same gain.

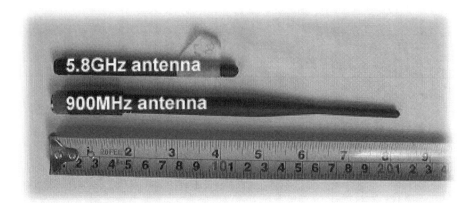

Figure 5.4 Size of Antenna

Environment also plays a role in network performance, as anyone watching satellite TV on a rainy day knows. Manufacturers advertise *line of sight* range figures. Line of sight means that from antenna-A you can see antenna-B. Being able to see the building that antenna B is in does not count as line of sight. For every obstacle in the path, de-rate the line of sight figure specified for each. The type, location and number of obstacles all play a role in path loss.

Application Layer

Perhaps one of the largest areas of competition in the IoT space is at the application layer, and in making it easy to connect new machines and pull data into a variety of collection architectures, which we'll discuss in the next chapter. Whether you're building a coffee pot or a generator, you're faced with a number of implementation decisions. Some have counted more than 100 suppliers. With such a large number of end applications to target, and such broad technology and data needs in terms of the platform, the number of players is not surprising. Some of the newer players include companies like Arrayent, Ayla Networks and Electric Imp. These companies have focused on lower cost and consumer machines including water heaters, postage stamp meters, washing machines, garage-door openers and medical wearables.

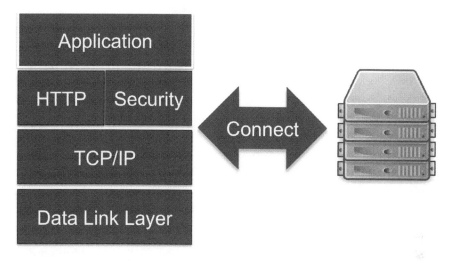

Figure 5.4 Application Layer

Some companies have been more focused on vertical markets, like Silver Spring Networks in the power industry. Silver Spring provides the ZigBee radio technology as well as higher-level connection protocols. Smaller players, like Axeda and 2lemtry, have been acquired by larger players — PTC and Amazon — and made part of a larger IoT framework.

Furthermore, there have been more traditional suppliers like Appareo, which supplies technology to AGCO. Appareo also makes its connection solutions backward compatible to support older farm equipment with the added ability to deal with harsher environments than found in the home environment. Some of these companies will also package cellular plans as part of the complete solution. ZTR, which got its start in train control, is a good example.

Network Security

Network security starts with authenticating, commonly with a username and password. This is called one-factor authentication. But with increased attention to security, many are implementing two-factor authentication, which requires the use of something the person physically owns. This could be a special-purpose device or, as many of you have seen, a cell phone that receives codes from the application to verify your identity a second time.

Once authenticated, firewalls enforce access policies such as what services are accessible by the network users. A firewall monitors and controls the incoming and outgoing network traffic based on a set of security rules; they typically establish a barrier between a trusted, secure internal network and another outside network, such as the Internet, that is assumed to be unsecure or untrusted.

Increasingly, firewalls also check for potentially harmful content such as computer worms or Trojans being transmitted over the network. Anti-virus software or intrusion prevention systems help detect and inhibit the action of such bad software. Network traffic may also be logged for audit purposes and later high-level analysis.

Finally, at the connection level, encryption is used to protect the transmitted data, as there is no way to physically secure the connection and prevent an attacker from being able to see the transmission. Encryption relies on a set of keys shared between the transmitter and the receiver. It also assumes that brute force attacks of trying every key will not be successful without massive computer resources. While encrypting transmissions can provide additional security, access control of the keys now becomes equally important.

As threats increase and Things and computers are increasingly networked and thereby accessible, there continues to be many innovations in the field of security.

6

Connect in Practice

Connecting Things requires a diverse set of technologies based on the amount of data that needs to be transmitted, how far it needs to go, how much power you have to consume and how big the antenna is. In this chapter, we'll focus on the wide variety of connection technologies implemented across a number of industries.

ZigBee

SensiumVitals is a wireless system designed to monitor the vital signs of patients in general wards. The system uses a lightweight, wearable, wireless, single-patient-use patch that wirelessly communicates vital signs to clinicians via a hospital's IT infrastructure. Today, the patches transmit data every two minutes, which is about 4,320 data points per patient, per day.

The patch is connected to the network with the ZigBee protocol; ZigBee is an IEEE 802.15.4-based specification for a suite of high-level communication protocols used to create personal area networks with small, low-power digital radios. The technology is intended to be simpler and less expensive than Bluetooth or WiFi. Its low-power consumption limits transmission distances to a line of sight of 10-100 meters.

The devices can transmit data over long distances by passing it through a mesh network of intermediate devices to reach more distant ones. ZigBee is typically used in low-data-rate applications that require long battery life and secure networking; 128-bit symmetric encryption keys secure the networks. ZigBee has a defined rate of 250 Kbit per second.

SensiumVitals has created a disposable sensor designed for five-day use for around $50. SensiumVitals actually uses a proprietary radio frequency to communicate that gives it its five-day battery life. This is compared to some WiFi solutions that cost 50 times more and require you to clean the product before using it with another patient.

SensiumVitals has implemented a bridge to connect the patches to the hospital server. Unlike with Bluetooth, this enables the patch wearer to move around without breaking the connection. A typical ward in a hospital might require 10 bridges.

WiFi

Most of you are familiar with WiFi technology, which has been the preferred mechanism to connect people to the Internet from offices to Starbucks. WiFi can reach up to 100 feet and can support hundreds of Megabits per second. Compared to ZigBee and

Bluetooth, WiFi consumes a lot of power, but that said, it is used extensively in office settings.

Pitney Bowes is connecting mail inserters to the Internet through a Cisco 819 Integrated Services Router. For each mail-manufacturing site, one Cisco device is used and placed on the network segment for the customers' fleet of mail inserters.

The Cisco 819 Integrated Services Router is the smallest Cisco IOS software router with support for integrated wireless WAN and wireless LAN capabilities. The Cisco 819 also has a virtual machine capability to support the execution of software developed by Pitney Bowes. This software checks the contents of files before they are pushed to GE's Predix platform. This white listing ensures that no Personally Identifiable Information (PII) is transmitted. Log files are created that allow Pitney Bowes and its clients to view and block content.

Data is transferred via a secure Transport Layer Security (TLS) connection. TLS and its predecessor, Secure Sockets Layer (SSL), both of which are frequently referred to as 'SSL', are cryptographic protocols designed to provide communications security over a network. Several versions of the protocols are in widespread use in applications such as web browsing, email, Internet faxing, instant messaging and voice over IP (VoIP). Major websites including Google, YouTube and Facebook use TLS to secure all communications between their servers and web browsers.

LoRaWAN

Wireless solutions have traditionally only had a few different technologies that they could rely on for communication. They could accept the limited range of standards-based local area technologies (e.g., WiFi, ZigBee and Bluetooth), or pay the costs for wide-area cellular technology. A new market is now emerging with the deployment of Low Power Wide Area Networks (LPWAN). These technologies hope to bridge the gap between current LAN and WAN technologies to allow for low-cost machine connections.

LPWAN specification is designed for wireless, battery-powered Things. The network architecture is typically laid out in a star-of-stars topology in which gateways relay messages between end-devices and a central network server in the backend. Gateways are connected to the network server via standard IP connections while end-devices use single-hop wireless communication to one or many gateways. All end-point communication is generally bi-directional but also supports operations such as multicast, enabling software upgrades over the air or other mass distribution messages to reduce the on-air communication time.

Communication between end-devices and gateways is spread out on different frequency channels and data rates. The selection of the data rate is a tradeoff between range and message duration. Due to the technology, communications with different data rates do not interfere with each other and create a set of virtual channels increasing the capacity of the gateway.

LoRaWAN data rates range from 0.3kbps to 50kbps. LoRaWAN's use of lower frequency (sub-GHz bands) means the signals can penetrate the core of large structures and subsurface deployments within a range of 2km.

Tata Communications (Tata) has announced plans for an India-wide LoRaWAN network following successful trials in Mumbai and Delhi. They join several other major telcos in adopting the technology. Orange has plans for a France-wide network and Telstra has begun early trials in Melbourne, Australia. LoRaWAN-technology pioneer, Semtech Corporation, has been selected by Tata to deploy the network with full coverage planned for Mumbai, Delhi and Bangalore.

Satellite

While there is increasing penetration of cellular and other technologies, many machines operate outside of that coverage. This is particularly true in rural areas around the world. As a result, satellite transmission remains one way to talk to the machine.

For example, locomotives can often be without WiFi or cellular connectivity. In response, GE manufactures the LOCOCOMM, a Communications Management Unit (CMU) applicable to both GE and non-GE locomotives. It uses an Intel single-board computer with 256MB of memory and up to 4GB of flash storage running a Microsoft Windows NT operating system. The system operates with no external cooling and is powered directly by a 74-volt locomotive battery.

In addition to communications, the CMU contains an integrated Global Positioning System (GPS) that provides a Differential Global Positioning System — an enhancement to GPS that provides improved location accuracy from the 15-meter nominal accuracy to about 10 centimeters in the best implementations. The unit uses satellite for small amounts of time-sensitive data and larger files are transferred over WiFi when the train reaches its destination.

Cellular Network

If you need a secure and reliable mobile connection between your Things and most of the countries in the world, Vodafone can provide that network. They achieve this by combining their mobile operations in 26 countries with partnerships in 55 others. In addition, they leverage these multiple network connections to ensure a much higher degree of availability and performance by providing multiple-path routing so that even a pacemaker can have a guaranteed level of connection service around the world.

Vodafone leverages a unique combination of global footprint augmented by strategic operator relationships outside of the operating companies, which is further augmented by more than 600 roaming partnerships. Vodafone combines this massive footprint with a global SIM providing a single means (SKU) for products to be distributed worldwide.

Furthermore, a single global support system provides a one-stop solution. This is all managed by a dedicated global M2M platform (called GDSP or Global Data Services Platform). Vodafone has mobile operations in 26 countries, partners with mobile networks in 55 more, and fixed broadband operations in 17 markets.

Firewalls

Because oil and gas platforms are within line of site of land, most of the traditional communication has been via microwave. Modern, bigger platforms are all connected by fiber optic cable. On the platform itself, the network interconnects a large quantity of programmable logic controllers (PLCs), instrumentation, smart, automated equipment and packaged, process-control equipment. In addition, the platform communicates with subsea systems and virtual flow meters using the OPC classic protocol.

Consequently, there is the potential for large amounts of network traffic and crosstalk. Some of the automation controllers deployed on the platform use a UDP broadcast/multicast protocol, which can further increases the volume of network traffic. Because many automation and control devices cannot filter out extraneous network messages, it can be necessary to protect those devices from excessive traffic.

A platform typically involves a myriad of contractors working on inter-related systems. At some point the network can be exposed to a computer virus, which have been known to come from infected USB drives from an unwitting contractor.

To protect the facility, some platforms implement an architecture that isolates layers of the business and process control network. The automation and business networks can be isolated using managed switches and logical network segregation. Demilitarized zones (DMZ) may be used to protect the process control system from the Internet and from the business network.

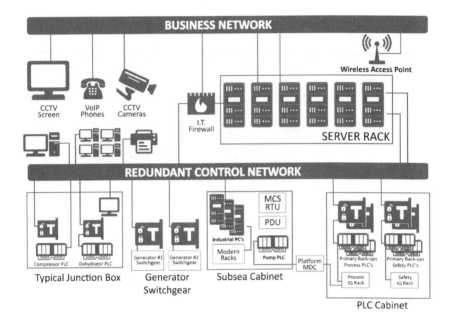

Figure 6.1 Connection Security

Figure 6.1 shows a deployment on one oil and gas platform. Belden's Tofino security appliance was installed in front of redundant Allen-Bradley Controllogix PLCs. The security appliances were configured and tested to ensure that the failover of the primary PLC processor to the backup processer would not impact control communications. In turn, the security appliances needed to maintain their security functionality regardless of the switchover state of the PLCs.

Next

Almost all of our communications hardware and software was built to connect people to the Internet. Things are not people. Things can tell you much more than people and can talk constantly. We have developed streaming technology to transmit large amounts of information (movies, games, etc.) from servers to people. Our next challenge will be to develop reverse streaming technology from Things back to the server. As we can control the rate of data transmission, there is the potential to make these reverse streaming networks efficient. As with streaming, we can afford to drop a few bits, but what will the network topology and control be like when 100,000 machines want to talk every minute? Some argue we should put more intelligence at the machines and send less data. But if we have a low-cost way to collect the data and can learn from our Things, why not send the data?

Finally, rather than security being an after thought (as it has been for IoP applications), we have the potential to engineer protected networks to communicate with these Things. Being able to authenticate the machines, control access, audit and protect the information as it flows is going to be important. With Things, it's likely that we'll need to be able to segregate machine data (data that describes the state of the machine such as its operating temperature and battery level) from *nomic* data (data that describes what the machine is measuring, such as properties of soil or blood); knowing the state of the blood analyzer or the gene sequencer (the *machine* data) will have different rules than knowing the blood analysis or gene sequence of an individual (*nomic* data). This brings us to the next step in the stack — collection.

7

Collect Principles

Things aren't people. One of the ways that's true is that the sheer volume of data that Things can generate is much greater than that of IoP applications. In this chapter we'll cover some fundamental ways that Thing data might be collected and stored. This includes SQL, noSQL and time-series collection architectures. And while we all might hope that all data of interest is stored in one way, the reality is that we live in a heterogeneous world. As a result, some technologies have evolved to process data from multiple SQL databases, for both structured and unstructured data. Finally, while much of today's data is collected in on-premises servers, cloud computing offers both a lower cost and higher quality alternative.

SQL RDBMS

SQL, which stands for Structured Query Language, is a special-purpose programming language designed for managing data in a relational database management system (RDBMS). Just like Excel tables, relational database tables consist of columns and rows. Each column contains a different type of attribute and each row corresponds to a single record. The structure of the database is often referred to as the schema.

Databases are much more powerful than spreadsheets in the way you can manipulate data, for example:

- Retrieve all records that match certain criteria
- Update records in bulk
- Cross reference records in different tables

There are many implementations of an RDBMS. For instance, to improve performance by leveraging the decreasing cost of memory, engineering efforts have gone into building in-memory databases (versus running on disk storage).

On the other hand, databases that run on disk storage can often experience improved performance by running in large memory caches, which again use the idea that memory access times are significantly faster than disk-access times.

In response, companies like SanDisk have pioneered the use of flash memory to eliminate the need for rotational disk storage. If you've bought a Mac Air in the past few years you might have noticed that the entire disk storage is solid state, meaning the old spinning disk is no where to be found. Managing hierarchies of storage based on performance and cost has occupied the industry for years and shows no signs of changing.

Finally, SQL databases are often characterized by the implementation of ACID properties. ACID stands for Atomicity, Consistency, Isolation and Durability. These are a series of properties born to serve the needs of transaction-processing applications.

One of the best use cases of ACID properties is debit-credit. For example, in a transaction-processing application, let's say you debit one account $1,000 and credit the other account $1,000. In this case, the bank wants to make sure that in the event of a failure during the transaction (e.g., software, operator or hardware failure), the results stored in the database are in a consistent state. In other words, a failure doesn't result in zero dollars in both accounts. This feature of SQL is used extensively in almost all IoP applications.

NoSQL

A NoSQL (originally referring to "non SQL" or "non relational") database provides a mechanism for storage and retrieval of data that is modeled in means other than the tabular relations used in relational databases. Motivations for this approach include schema-less, simplicity of design and simpler horizontal scaling to clusters of machines. The data structures used by NoSQL databases (e.g., key-value, graph or document) differ slightly from those used by default in relational databases, making some operations faster in NoSQL and others faster in relational databases.

Most NoSQL databases lack ACID transactions. Instead they offer a concept of *eventual consistency*, in which database changes are eventually propagated to all nodes (typically within milliseconds) so queries for data might not return updated data immediately.

Applications where SQL is better:
- Logical, related or discrete data requirements that can be identified up-front
- Data integrity is essential
- Standards-based proven technology with wide developer experience

Applications where NoSQL is better:
- Unrelated, indeterminate or evolving data requirements
- Simpler or looser project objectives that enable coding efforts to start immediately
- Speed and scalability is imperative

Time Series

Let's now move to thinking more specifically about collecting data from machines. Machines can deliver data once per hour, minute, second or many times per second. That data could be voltage levels from a generator, CO_2 level from a gas sensor or the number of revolutions per second of a wind turbine.

The fundamental challenge in using a SQL RDBMS for time-series data is how to treat each sample from the time-series within the database. Is a unique sample a unique row in a table with columns of time-stamp and sensor value? If you only had 1,000 machines, each with a ten-sensors sampling at 20 times per second that would generate more than 17 billion rows per day. If you were a disk-storage company you'd be happy, but most users would be concerned with the cost and performance implications.

As a result, a number of companies have built time-series databases, sometimes referred to as *historians*. These products include PI from OSISoft, Proficy Historian from GE, IP21 from AspenTech and eDNA and Wonderware from Schneider.

A real-time historian is like a flight recorder for process data. Rather than relational, it is a temporal database that stores its records in a flat file consisting of simply the name, value, quality and timestamp for a data point. The historian is designed for speed of storage and retrieval of data, and can typically process millions of events per second. Most of these databases have designed some types of data compression to reduce the cost of archiving large amounts of time-series data.

As you can guess, there are debates between the SQL RDBMS groups and the time-series folks. Time-series database advocates will declare they are able to compress time-series data by a factor of 5,000 versus traditional RDBMS implementations. On the other hand, those who advocate RDBMS solutions declare that there are far more programmers and support, and disk storage is becoming lower cost all the time.

As with traditional RDBMS technology, the open source community is bringing many other technologies into focus. Some IoT companies, including Ayla and Arrayent, are using Cassandra, which was developed by Facebook to store time-series data. OpenTSDB is another open source effort in the area.

Heterogeneous Data

Hadoop
Hadoop is a software technology designed for storing and processing large volumes of data distributed across a cluster of commodity servers and commodity storage. In the early 2000s, Google published papers outlining its approach and design principles to handling large volumes of data as it indexed the Web. These papers heavily influenced the development of Hadoop. Three of those fundamental design principals are:

- First, given hundreds or even thousands of storage machines, failures are the norm rather than the exception; therefore, constant monitoring, error detection, fault tolerance and automatic recovery must be integral to the system.

- Second, files are huge by traditional standards. Multi-GB files and billions of objects are common. As a result, design assumptions and parameters such as I/O operation and block sizes have to be revisited.

- Third, most files are updated by appending new data rather than overwriting existing data. Random writes within a file are practically non-existent. Once written, the files are read-only and often only read sequentially. Given this access pattern on huge files, appending becomes the focus of performance optimization and atomicity guarantees.

Initially, Hadoop consisted of a distributed file system called HDFS and a data processing and execution model called MapReduce. HDFS is a distributed file system that stores data on commodity machines, providing high-aggregate bandwidth across the cluster. MapReduce allows the programmer to create parallel programs to process the data.

In addition to these base modules, the term Hadoop has evolved to also include a host of tools that can be installed on top of or alongside Hadoop to simplify access and processing of data. These include: HBase, a NoSQL, distributed database modeled after Google's BigTable; Hive, a data-warehouse infrastructure providing SQL-like access to data; Pig, a scripting language for accessing and transforming data; Mahout, a machine learning library and Spark, an in-memory cluster-computing framework used for fast-batch processing, event streaming and interactive queries; some think of Spark as a potential successor to MapReduce.

Splunk

Splunk came from a very different problem space than indexing and searching the Web, which drove much of the early work on Hadoop. It was instead designed for system administrators to analyze log files generated by a system's hardware or software.

While a database requires you to define tables and fields before you can store data, Splunk accepts almost anything because it does not have a fixed schema. Instead, it performs field extraction at search time; this approach allows for greater flexibility. Just as Google crawls any Web page without knowing anything about a site's layout, Splunk indexes any kind of machine data that can be represented as text.

During the indexing phase, when Splunk processes incoming data and prepares it for storage, the indexer makes one significant modification — it chops up the stream of characters into individual events. Events typically correspond to lines in the log file being processed. Each event gets a timestamp, typically pulled directly from the input line, and a few other default properties like the originating machine. Then event keywords are added to an index file to speed up later searches. Splunk stores data directly in the file system, which is great from a scalability and reliability point of view.

Although you can just use simple search terms like a username to see how often that turns up in a given time period, Splunk's Search Processing Language (SPL) allows you to do more. For example, you might want to know which applications are the slowest to start up, making the end user wait the longest. By using a combination of SPL and Unix-like Pipe commands, you can discover the answer.

Splunk can run on HDFS with a product they call Hunk. Also, as you can guess, there are now some open source alternatives including Graylog, which is written in Java and uses a few open source technologies: Elasticsearch (a distributed, multitenant capable full-text search engine), MongoDB (a NoSQL cross-platform document-oriented database) and Apache Kafka (a messaging broker system that allows streamed data to be partitioned across a cluster of machines and has many big data analysis applications).

Cloud Computing

Much of the data collected today continues to be the traditional, on-premises model that's custom managed by a team of people; the advent of cloud computing promises to both reduce cost but also increase the overall quality of service. Several years ago, Amazon CEO, Jeff Bezos, announced the availability of compute and storage cloud services called EC2 and S3. In 2015, Amazon announced it had reached over $6 billion in revenue. Cloud computing is first and foremost a business model based on a new economic model and driven by technology.

The predominate cost of compute and storage is not the cost of the boxes or even the racks they fit in; instead, it's the cost of managing the security, availability, performance and change of the compute and storage environment. As a simple example, any secure compute and storage infrastructure needs to make sure that every applicable vendor security patch is applied. Being aware of those patches, testing them and applying them to the environment requires human labor. Conservatively, the cost to manage infrastructure is at least four times the purchase price per year. In four years, you're spending 16 times the purchase price to manage the boxes — so the cost of the boxes is a relatively small percentage of the overall costs.

To address this high infrastructure management cost, cloud service providers can dedicate engineering resources to automate the key processes to manage the security, availability and performance of the compute and storage environments. Through automation, they can both dramatically reduce the cost and increase the overall quality of service. Because as some of us know, the biggest single source of failure in operational systems is human error.

Let's now look at a few of these collections implemented in IoT applications across a few industries.

8

Collect in Practice

Once machines, assets or devices are connected, there are a variety of ways the data can be collected. In *Collect Principles* we outlined SQL, noSQL and time-series databases as some of the fundamental technologies used today. While it would be ideal to have just one database of record, in practice this is never the case. As a result, a variety of technologies including Hadoop and Splunk have emerged to process data from multiple sources. In this chapter, we'll take some of the collection principles and see how they're applied in practice in construction, oil and gas, power and healthcare.

Construction

More and more, construction equipment rental companies are becoming digital to increase the level of service and decrease the cost to deliver machines to their clients. With assets valued in the billions, small changes can make a big difference.

One of the largest construction-rental companies uses a third-party supplier to instrument, connect and collect data from their equipment in the field. Once per hour, data from the third-party provider is delivered into an enterprise resource planning (ERP) application. In this case, a specialized application called Rental Man is used. As with most ERP apps, it runs on a SQL database. Furthermore, data is also exported to a Teradata database that serves as a data warehouse for analysis.

Water

As many water-service companies do, Moundsville Wastewater Treatment Plant (Moundsville) in West Virginia uses lagoon tanks. Lagoon tanks are holding ponds that are artificially aerated to promote oxidation as part of treating wastewater. As part of an upgrade, Kaeser Compressors Inc. (Kaeser), a compressed-air-systems company, installed a new blower and sensors to control airflow in two new tanks. As a result, Moundsville is saving approximately 50–60 thousand dollars per year in energy costs. To better monitor operations onsite and improve customer service, Kaeser uses SAP's HANA SQL database to collect the data and a custom-built predictive maintenance application to avoid unplanned downtime. With a better understanding of its machines and the ability to analyze them continuously, Kaeser has now taken the next step and sells air by the cubic meter through compressors it owns and maintains.

Yorkshire Water provides clean water and wastewater treatment services to 4.7 million people and 130,000 businesses in Northern England. The company also manages 650 water storage facilities, 2,250 pumping stations and 86 wastewater treatment facilities. Measurements of water pressure, flow volume, pump state, reservoir level and water quality are all gathered from sensors throughout the enterprise. As the customer base grew, so did the amount of data it was collecting. Yorkshire Water has implemented applications based on OSISoft's PI system, one of the earliest time-series databases; they were able to reduce cost by shifting energy-intensive activities, like pumping sewage at night when energy costs are lower, and as a result have saved £900,000 annually.

Power

Silver Spring Networks, a provider of smart-grid infrastructure, has created CustomerIQ, an application that analyzes utility meter data in MongoDB, a noSQL collection technology. MongoDB allows the aggregation of utility meter data, weather data, enterprise customer information systems, rate plan structure and pricing information. Consumer Energy, a public utility in Michigan, has connected four million meters. Meter data is read multiple times a day and receives customer account record changes in real time. MongoDB was deployed as a cloud service at Amazon Web Services (AWS) so there was no fixed infrastructure cost and the management of the security, availability and performance of the compute and storage is left to Amazon.

Using MongoDB, Silver Spring Networks developed an application that provides real-time analysis of energy usage breakdowns and costs for consumers and enterprises. Customers with solar-power generation can have real-time savings estimates with the energy produced cycled back into the grid, which gives the utility insight into the impact of the energy grid's stability. At Oklahoma Gas and Electric, consumers get an updated energy forecast every 30 minutes and can have their thermostat adjusted to save costs during critical peak-pricing hours for energy.

Many power companies use General Electric turbines to generate electricity. Pivotal GemFire, a distributed, in-memory data grid, enables GE's Monitoring & Diagnostics (M&D) Center to ingest and store 100,000 time-series data points. The M&D Center is located in Atlanta, Georgia and collects more than 30,000 operating hours of data from a fleet of more than 1,500 gas-turbine and generator machines, supplementing a 40-terabyte database representing more than 100 million operating hours. The M&D team of more than 50 engineers analyzes upwards of 35,000 operational alarms per year. Among the sensors monitored at the center are the inlet temperature of a compressor, thermal performance of a gas turbine, temperature of combustion exhaust, vibration levels of a rotor and the temperature of bearings. The M&D Center serves more than 500 customer sites, providing assisted services to power plant customers in more than 50 countries.

Renewable energy is becoming an increasingly important part of the power industry. The Spanish company 9REN operates 568 photovoltaic power plants primarily in Spain and Italy. In total, they generate more than 99,000-megawatt hours of electrical power every year. To manage and monitor its photovoltaic plant facilities, 9REN created a solution built on Schneider Electric software. The application runs on five servers — a pair that controls the plants in Spain and another two controlling operations in Italy. The fifth is for historic information and operates the Wonderware historian database designed to collect a wide variety of time-series plant data.

While much is happening on the production end of the power industry, enterprises are also implementing IoT applications to manage consumption. McKenney's, also in Georgia, implemented a Splunk solution to manage power at Eglin Air Force Base (Eglin). Here, HVAC data is collected in 15-minute increments and power-meter data is collected continuously in real-time by Sensus. Sensus-meter data is collected in a Microsoft SQL server database then passed to the Splunk indexer. Splunk also collects information from flat files that can be manually input, as well as log files from the Niagara AX system and InterMapper server. Eglin's implementation is projected to save millions of dollars in energy costs.

Healthcare

Once data is collected it needs to be processed. As we discussed in the previous chapter, Hadoop is increasingly being used to process unstructured and structured data. One example in the healthcare industry is the use of SensiumVitals patches to continuously monitor a patient's vital signs — heart rate, respiration rate and temperature – – with a high degree of accuracy. Today the patches transmit data every two minutes, which is about 4,320 data points per patient, per day. A major hospital used Hadoop because it was a simple solution that allowed data to be ingested in its native form. By combining data from both the patch and EMR systems, they are trying to use data and constant monitoring to improve patient outcomes and reduce costs.

Financial Services

Progressive launched its Snapshot usage-based insurance program in 2008. The dongle, which plugs into the OBD-II diagnostic port, collects data on how many miles are driven, what times of day a vehicle is in operation and how hard a driver brakes. In exchange for this data, good drivers can receive discounts off their premiums as big as 30%. Among other data, the vehicles can provide run-time data such as engine start, barometric pressure, accelerator pedal position, hybrid battery pack remaining life, engine-oil temperature and turbocharger RPM.

Progressive started collecting data from Snapshot devices but initially the high cost of ETL transformations and storage meant that they actually only stored 25% of the available data streaming from cars. Now, after adopting Hadoop, they are able to store all of that driving data, which today represents more than 10 billion miles driven. The drivers who opt-in to the Snapshot program have online access to the data they generate at the end of each trip, using their Progressive policy account to get visualized reports.

Next

Collection technology will be challenged in the future; we're going to need to devise both lower cost ways to store data coming from Things, as well as faster processing architectures.

Just to get a sense of scale, suppose you have 100,000 machines in the field. For instance, a large construction rental company has over 425,000 machines deployed and Vestas, the largest wind turbine manufacturer, has at least 50,000 machines in the field. Let's assume today you're only sampling data once per hour and the amount of data is just 100 bytes. At that rate you'll generate 0.24GB of data per day, or 87GB per year. Let's assume you collect this data in a traditional – – Oracle, Microsoft, Pivotal, IBM, Teradata — database. If you took the average of the total cost of ownership of these five solutions from a recent report,[1] the cost of collecting the data would be approximately $16,000 per GB. For our IoT application, that would amount to $1.44 million.

Now let's suppose we keep the same number of machines but increase the data-sampling rate to once per minute. Again, this is not a wild assumption, as wind turbines today sample once every 5-10 seconds. Furthermore, let's assume we have more sophisticated

---

[1] Microsoft Analytics Platform System Delivers Best TCO-to-Performance, published by: Value Prism Consulting; sponsored by: Microsoft Corporation, published September 2014

sensors that now deliver 1,000 bytes of data. With just these two changes, the volume of data now moves to 144GB per day, and in a year to 52,560GB (or 52 Terabytes). At the same cost structures of about $16,000 per GB, a traditional collection approach would round out to $861 million for five years. This of course is if we only keep the data for one year and there are no new machines.

No matter how you cut it, clearly we're going to need much lower cost alternatives. But it's not just going to be about cost; traditional sequential techniques won't be adequate to process 52 Terabytes. Of course, the first question we might want to ask is how are we going to use the data? For the first time, we're going to get a lot of data without having to entice people to type — so what will we be able to learn?

9

Learn Principles

With an increasing amount of data coming from Things, we'll need to apply technology to learn from the data. In this chapter, we'll cover some major areas including query technology, supervised and unsupervised machine learning and clustering.

At a high level, machine-learning algorithms can be divided into two distinct categories — supervised and unsupervised learning. Supervised-learning algorithms learn a predictive model that maps an input pattern to a desired output value. To train the predictive model in a supervised manner, we must use a set of training data consisting of input patterns together with the desired output values for each input pattern. The learning process is described as "supervised" because the predictive model is provided with supervisory information in the form of the true output values that it needs to predict during training.

In contrast, unsupervised learning is concerned with finding clusters in a set of input data and does not require any output values to be present in the dataset. Because, as an industry, we have mostly focused on IoP applications, most of the technology applied to learning from data streams has been applied to learning from data about people. In this chapter, we'll cover some of these basic concepts, some of which will apply to Things.

Database Query

A query is a specific request for a subset of data or for statistics about data, formulated in a technical language, and posted to a database system. Many tools are available to answer one-off or repeating queries about data posed by a worker. These tools are usually front ends to database systems, based on Structured Query Language (SQL) or a tool with a graphical user interface (GUI) to help formulate queries. For example, a query could answer the question: "Where are the most 100KW generators in the Northeast?"

Database queries are appropriate when you already have an idea of what might be an interesting subpopulation of the data and want to investigate this population or confirm a hypothesis about the data. In contrast, data mining could be used to come up with this query in the first place as a pattern or regularity in the data.

On-line Analytical Processing (OLAP) provides a GUI to query large data collections for the purpose of facilitating data exploration. Unlike the "ad-hoc" querying enabled by tools like SQL, the dimensions of analysis for OLAP must be pre-programmed into the OLAP system. Unlike with OLAP, data-mining tools generally incorporate new dimensions of analysis easily as part of the exploration. OLAP tools can be a useful complement to data-mining tools for discovery from business data.

Prediction

At its most general, prediction is concerned with the task of estimating one or more desired quantities of interest (the "output values") given a number of input-data values, which are typically represented as a fixed-size vector. The job of the predictive model is to provide a mapping from the input-data vector to the desired output value(s). This mapping takes the form of a mathematical function, which is governed by a set of parameters, or weights. The job of the learning algorithm is to find the optimal set of parameters such that the predictive model is able to generate accurate predictions of the output values for each input vector that it's presented with.

The output values we wish to predict may be either continuous or discrete in nature. If the outputs are continuous values then the prediction problem is known as *regression* (the predictive model is known as a *regression model*). If the outputs are discrete values, then the prediction problem is known as *classification* (the predictive model is known as a *classifier*). To illustrate this further, consider two possible prediction problems when designing algorithms for a wearable fitness band. Predicting the heart rate of the user — a continuous value — would require a regression model. Conversely, predicting whether the user's heart-rate patterns were normal (class 0) or abnormal (class 1) would require a classifier.

Prediction, whether in the form of regression or classification, requires a *labeled* dataset to learn from. In a labeled dataset, each example is an input-output pair consisting of the input vector together with the desired output value (label). A supervised-learning algorithm uses this dataset to optimize the parameters of the predictive model, such that the model provides good predictive performance on new data. In order to assess the model's likely performance on new data, the labeled dataset is typically partitioned into a training set and a test set. The training set is then used to optimize the model parameters using a supervised learning algorithm; and the test set is used to assess the model performance once training has completed.

Novelty Detection

Although predictive modeling is a powerful technique, there are problems where we would like to make a prediction about the *state* of a system, but where we are unable to apply the standard prediction techniques described in the previous section.

As an illustrative example, consider the task of predicting the health of a jet engine during flight. This type of problem is often referred to as *health monitoring* or *condition monitoring*. Specifically, we are tasked with building an algorithm that can predict if an engine is operating normally or, alternatively, operating in a novel or abnormal way that may indicate a problem within the engine. To approach this as a standard prediction problem, we would first collect a labeled dataset consisting of examples of jet engines operating normally (class 0) together with examples of engines operating abnormally (class 1). Given this dataset, we could then train a classifier in a supervised manner to decipher normal from abnormal engine behavior.

However, when we try to take this approach we quickly encounter a fundamental problem. What if we only have access to a very small number of examples of engines operating abnormally? In the extreme case, for a new model of a well-designed jet engine, we may not have any examples of the engine operating abnormally. In this scenario, our labeled dataset then consists solely of examples of engines operating normally.

Furthermore, even if we can obtain some examples of engines operating abnormally, we are still left with a problem; perhaps in the future, a fault may develop in some engines after many years of use that is quite different in nature to the abnormal examples present in our training set. So, we would like to be able to *detect* if an engine is operating abnormally, even when we may never have seen examples of this type of abnormal engine behavior during training.

The solution to this problem is a technique called *novelty* or *anomaly detection*. The key insight of the novelty detection approach is to focus exclusively on the *normal* data (i.e. the available data about the system behaving normally). Therefore, instead of trying to build a classifier to decipher normal from abnormal, we first build a model of only normal data. Then, using our "normality model," we test new input data against this model and evaluate the probability or likelihood that the data is indicative of the system operating normally (i.e. that the input data could have been generated by the normality model with high probability). If the normality model assigns high probability to the input data, we can be confident that the system is behaving normally; however, if the normality model assigns low probability to the data, then this is indicative of a potential problem because the input data is quite different from that which the model was trained on. The power of this technique is that we are potentially able to detect novel or anomalous events in the data generated by complex systems — such as jet engines — when we may have never previously encountered examples of such events.

Clustering

Clustering is a set of techniques for discovering patterns or "clusters" within input data. A cluster is defined as a collection of input data vectors that are similar according to some metric. Most commonly, clusters refer to distinct regions of the input data space that have a high density of input data vectors such that the input vectors within each cluster can be considered to belong to some distinct underlying class or group. So, clustering is best viewed as a technique for discovering "groupings" within a dataset, which may not be readily apparent by computing simple, statistical summaries of the data.

Clustering is a form of unsupervised learning because it only uses the input-data vectors and does not make use of any labels or output values that we may have. It is distinct from novelty detection in that the aim of clustering is to discover groupings within the data where each grouping represents input patterns with high similarity; whereas the aim of novelty detection is to build a faithful statistical model of the full range of normal input data.

A common use case for clustering is as part of an exploratory data analysis (EDA). EDA is often performed as one of the initial steps of a machine-learning project. Even when the overall aim of the project is to build a predictive model or a novelty detection system, it is often helpful to begin with a clustering and visualization stage in order to understand patterns in the data that may be helpful for subsequent modeling efforts.

Dynamic Machine Learning

For many machine-learning problems, we can consider that each data object in our dataset is *statistically independent* of all the other data objects in the dataset. For example, if we wish to predict the price of houses given data about each house (e.g., lot size, bedrooms, zip code, etc.), we can consider that each house is independent of the next. More precisely, the data about any given house does not provide useful predictive information about any other house. Intuitively this makes sense — the number of bedrooms (or lot size, heating type, etc.) in one house is unlikely to influence the price of another.

By treating the data — houses in this case — as independent of each other, we can represent each object by a fixed-size-feature vector and treat the set of feature vectors across all the data objects as independent of one another. This leads to conceptually simple machine-learning models that simply take a feature vector as input for a given data object and compute a desired value of interest (e.g., class label, novelty score or cluster assignment).

However, for some important problems we cannot take the above approach. For example, when analyzing a stream of time-series data from a sensor, we must take into account the temporal patterns across the data in order to achieve optimal performance. If we attempt to "window" the time series to create a sequence of fixed-size-feature vectors that can be fed into a standard machine-learning model (e.g., a classifier), we are faced with a number of challenges such as how large to make our window (bigger = more data for the features; smaller = better temporal resolution), and how much to shift our window at each step. Furthermore, the resulting windowed feature vectors will likely exhibit significant correlations across one or more of the individual features; therefore, we need a way to model the statistical structure inherent in the time series. This is the domain of dynamic machine learning, which is concerned with the analysis of sequence or temporal data for which the standard independence assumptions inherent in many machine-learning algorithms do not apply.

For time-series prediction problems, autoregressive models (and derivatives such as ARMA and ARIMA) provide a simple but effective form of dynamic machine-learning algorithm. For the most challenging problems, state-space models such as Kalman Filters and Hidden Markov Models (HMMs) can give superior performance.

Learning Lifecycle

It is tempting to view the learning process as a software development cycle. Indeed, machine-learning projects are often treated and managed as engineering projects, which is understandable when they are initiated by software departments with data generated by a large software system and analytics results fed back into it. Managers are usually familiar with software technologies and are comfortable managing software projects; milestones can be agreed upon and success is usually unambiguous.

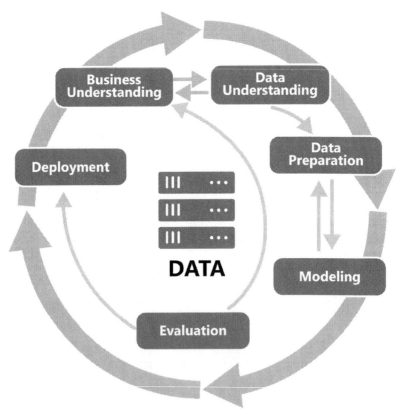

Figure 9.1 CRISP (Data Mining) Lifecycle

Software managers might look at the CRISP data-mining cycle (see Figure 9.1) and think it looks comfortably similar to a software-development cycle, so they should be right at home managing an analytics or learning project the same way. This can be a mistake because learning is an exploratory undertaking closer to research and development than it is to engineering. The CRISP cycle is based around exploration, iterating on approaches and strategy rather than software designs.

The task of determining a suitable representation of the raw input data that maximizes the performance of a machine-learning model is referred to as *feature engineering*, and the resulting data vector used as the input to the model is referred as a *feature vector*. Feature engineering is often one of the most important aspects of a machine-learning project. Coming up with good features that enable a machine-learning model to perform to a high standard on a given application requires a combination of exploratory data analysis, experimentation and often the use of prior knowledge about the system under study.

Outcomes are far less certain and the results of a given step may change the fundamental understanding of the problem. Engineering a learning or analytics solution directly for deployment can be an expensive, premature commitment. Instead, analytics projects should prepare to invest in information to reduce uncertainty in various ways. Small investments can be made via pilot studies and throwaway prototypes. Data scientists or machine-learning engineers should review the literature to see what else has been done and how it has worked. On a larger scale, a team can invest substantially in building experimental test beds to allow extensive agile experimentation. If you're a software manager, this will look more like research and exploration than you're used to, and maybe more than you're comfortable with.

Although machine learning involves software, it also requires skills that may not be common among programmers. In software engineering, the ability to write efficient, high-quality code from requirements may be paramount. Team members may be evaluated using software metrics, such as the amount of code written or number of bug tickets closed. In analytics, it's more important for individuals to be able to formulate problems well, prototype solutions quickly, make reasonable assumptions in the face of ill-structured problems, design experiments that represent good investments and analyze results. In building a data-science team, these qualities — rather than traditional software engineering expertise — are skills that should be sought.

10

Learn in Practice

In the *Learn Principles* chapter we covered a few fundamental ways you can learn from data from Things. Unlike the last generation of IoP applications, we don't have to wait for someone to buy a book or hire a new employee to have data to analyze. Machine-generated data is both richer (as we can have hundreds of sensors) and much more frequent (sometimes up to 60 times per second) than IoP data. As a result, there has been a great deal of work in technologies, such as supervised and unsupervised machine learning, clustering and engagement analysis. We're still in the early stages, but in this chapter we'll cover four examples of learning in practice.

Oil and Gas

In 2011, GE acquired SmartSignal, a Chicago-based company founded on patented technology that Argonne National Laboratory scientists developed in the early 1990s to predict pump failures at nuclear facilities. With SmartSignal, each Thing is modeled by its unique, historical data. The models put into context the normal operating relationships among all relevant parameters such as load, temperatures, pressures, vibration readings and ambient conditions. During the learning phase, a model of normal behavior is established. Once a model is created, the SmartSignal software detects and identifies events and abnormal behavior by the differences between real-time, actual data and predicted, normal behavior — not by thresholds on actual values.

Offshore oilrigs contain hundreds of machines. A few years ago, SmartSignal implemented the monitoring of a diesel generator; after a three-day outage, the generator was brought back online. Given the operating conditions, the pressure should have been around four BARG — the pressure, in units of bars, above or below atmospheric pressure. In this case, the actual oil pressure was 3.5 BARG and, based on SmartSignal's models, it predicted a failure. Luckily, the oilrig's operator had the opportunity to identify a faulty oil pump on the generator before the pump failed. This allowed them to avoid the costs of performing emergency repairs of the pump. In addition, if this pump had failed while operating, it would have tripped the generator offline. This loss of power could have forced the entire platform to reduce or cease production. In this case, implementing machine learning provided a more reliable diesel generator — a more precise machine.

Transportation

New York Air Brake (NYAB) provides train control systems to railroads, such as Norfolk Southern in the United States, as well as mining operators like Rio Tinto in Australia. With the ability to instrument trains, connect and collect the data, they are able to implement both supervised and unsupervised machine-learning algorithms.

NYAB has been providing brakes for trains for more than 100 years, so it makes sense that they would use data to provide predictive and prescriptive analytics of brake-shoe wear. NYAB can recreate train runs in simulation and determine how much energy was absorbed by the brake shoes on individual cars. This can then be compared to data models relating brake-shoe wear to the energy absorbed. Given the historical data of the car and the projected route, combined with historical simulation data of that route, NYAB can provide a prediction on how much wear a brake shoe will experience in its future travels.

NYAB uses supervised machine learning for fuel-efficiency analysis. Information like wind data, train length, number of stops required and efficiency of the locomotives are used as inputs into multivariable regressions. A time window is created based on seasonal changes in order to keep the data model current. Effectiveness of the model is used to determine potential for energy reduction of segments based on the R^2 (R squared) value. Fuel predictions from the model are used as the baseline to which new data is compared to quantify fuel savings. Norfolk Southern estimated a 5% fuel savings to their deployment, resulting in 10.8 million gallons of diesel fuel saved and the avoidance of more than 109,500 metric tons of greenhouse gas emissions.

NYAB is also using unsupervised machine learning to implement train-handling risk mitigation. Here they collect the location and the magnitude of the in-train forces along a route as well as information like the train's length, weight and weight distribution. Using this data, they can predict the likelihood that a train will experience handling issues. Based on what they learn, NYAB software can advise to slow the train over a particular section of track. Of course, if you can provide timely advice, you can also control the train remotely. NYAB is on track to power the world's first autonomous train bringing iron ore from Northern Australia to Perth on Rio Tinto's trains.

Power

Phasor measurement technology was introduced in the power industry more than 30 years ago but did not get much attention until the Northeast blackout of 2003, where it became clear that more detailed monitoring capabilities for the electricity grid were needed. Phasor measurement units (PMUs) take measurements at the power-frequency voltage, current and phasor angle (i.e. where you are on the power sine wave). Modern PMUs take readings at a speed of 60 times per second, while the previous systems only took readings every 3-4 seconds, resulting in over 200 times the amount of data. Considering there can be hundreds of these sensors in a grid, it's too much information for any operator to rationalize.

Duke Energy has deployed several hundred of these PMUs in the field and engaged SAS Enterprise Miner to learn from these measurements. The main purpose is to detect and understand events that are affecting the power grid, with the objective to keep the grid stable. Duke Energy has learned there are a number of time-series techniques that are needed. The analysis flow breaks down into three areas: event detection (did something happen?), event identification (what happened?) and event quantification (how bad was it?).

While there is a lot of data, fortunately a majority of the time nothing significant is occurring. In this case, time-series data can be modeled and used to detect when there is a deviation from the normal pattern. These models implemented in SAS allowed Duke to look forward with a very short-term forecast and detect an event of interest.

An event of interest doesn't necessarily mean there is a problem or that one will develop; some events are random, like a lightning strike or a tree hitting a power line, while others represent some type of equipment failure. Duke Energy has determined that many of these events produce a similar signature in the data stream. Time-series similarity analysis and time-series clustering have been able to match the incoming events to previously seen events. Tagging which previous event signatures are non-consequential allows them to safely ignore them.

The last challenge is event quantification, which asks the question: how bad is it? For some events, the question is whether or not the magnitude of the event gives cause for concern. One example is oscillation on the power grid; small but diminishing oscillations are not necessarily a problem, but larger ones that are increasing may require further attention.

To learn more, consider reading Kathleen Sico's master's degree dissertation at North Carolina State University[2], which goes into more detail on each of these subjects.

Healthcare

Over the past several years, there has been more discussion about precision healthcare. As healthcare costs rise, there is every incentive to employ computing to assist in reducing overall costs. As you think of this challenge in terms of global healthcare, it will be difficult if solutions are based only on highly trained healthcare professionals.

UC Irvine launched a project a few years ago to use a disposable monitor built by SensiumVitals to observe patients' vital signs. By using three years of historic sensor data coupled with Code Blue and

---

[2] http://repository.lib.ncsu.edu/ir/bitstream/1840.16/9899/1/etd.pdf

rapid-response events, the Irvine team built a predictive model. Code Blue is used to indicate a patient requiring resuscitation or in need of immediate medical attention, most often as the result of a respiratory or cardiac arrest. The model also used other sources of data including EMR and lab data. Other time-series data included the amount of oxygen in the blood, the partial pressure of carbon dioxide in arterial blood and blood-pressure measurement.

A team from Tata Consulting Services built the first models; using both ARIMA (Autoregressive Integrated Moving Average) models and support-vector machines written in R: ARIMA models are applied in cases where data shows evidence of non-stationarity. Support-vector machines are supervised-learning models with associated-learning algorithms that analyze data and recognize patterns used for classification and regression analysis. The result of their work was an ability to predict a Code Blue with reasonable accuracy within 90 seconds of the event. Of course, you need to make sure you don't cry wolf too often, referred to as the "false-positive rate." And, while a 90-second prediction into the future is a good start, their goal is to give a 10-minute prediction. Charles Boicey, who drove the work at UC Irvine, has gone on to ClearSense to continue the work.

Next

These examples should give you an idea of what some industries are doing today, but in many ways it's still very early. There is still debate over how much data we should collect; some are discussing collecting less data because they are faced with the high cost of data connection and collection, but numerous innovations promise to significantly change the economics. Our biggest challenge in learning from machine data is people, not technology. Based on some analysis of the machine-learning-class enrollment at Stanford and other

Universities over the past ten years, you can extrapolate there are probably only 10 thousand people in the world trained in any form of machine learning. Compare that number to an estimated 10 million software programmers worldwide and you'll get an idea of the challenges, and perhaps more importantly, the opportunities.

11

Do Principles

Outcomes — what are they? What does all of this technology to connect, collect and learn actually do? In this chapter, we'll discuss the value of higher degrees of service for machines, both to the producers and consumers of Things. As machines become more and more complex and increasingly enabled by software, many of the lessons learned in software maintenance and service will also apply to machine service. Finally, as many in the software industry already know, the movement to deliver software as a service has revolutionized the industry. We'll finish by talking about how those business models can reshape the business models for everyone building industrial products. These six outcomes are the business benefits for either the producers or consumers of modern machines. But before we do that let's discuss applications.

Enterprise Applications

Beginning in the late 1990s, a group of companies including PeopleSoft, Siebel, Oracle and SAP built enterprise applications on client/server architectures. These applications supported functions done by people in finance, accounting, sales, marketing and human resources. And starting in the 2000s, many new companies such as Salesforce.com, NetSuite, Concur, Taleo and SuccessFactors emerged delivering similar function as a cloud service. Specialized applications have also emerged, such as Veeva in pharmaceuticals, Dealertrack in automotive and Blackbaud in philanthropy. While all of these companies have been successful, packaged, enterprise applications cover a small percentage on what many enterprises do. A few years ago, I asked the CIO of 7-Eleven what percentage of the application footprint was bought from suppliers such as Microsoft or Oracle, and the answer was 10%.

Middleware

As a result, most enterprise applications are custom written. For example, 7-Eleven has a fuel-management application written for its gas stations. The term middleware has been classically used to describe a set of services or software that provides common functionality. A simple example is security services. All IoP applications need an authentication service to establish the identity of the individual. Managing passwords, ensuring they are changed and protecting them are all common functions, which every developer doesn't need to write. Another example is workflow or process management, where common software can be used to orchestrate a step-by-step sequence of actions. You see a simple example of this every time you check out with your purchases on Amazon.com.

While of course we could write a whole book on middleware, the intent of this chapter is to focus on some fundamental outcomes that would result from implementing an application. We'll begin with two important outcomes that a provider of mining, agriculture or healthcare machines might expect.

Precision Machines: Improve quality of service

In the computing industry, both hardware and software companies have traditionally provided maintenance services. In the case of software, this is typically priced as a percentage of the initial purchase price; this business model generates the most revenue and profit for the first generation of enterprise software companies (e.g., Oracle or SAP). Many years ago, computer hardware companies connected their computers so they could "phone home" and report any potential problems, thereby improving the quality of service.

Of course, the manufacturers of generators, blood analyzers and forklifts can do the same. By connecting their Things to the Internet, not only is there a potential additional revenue stream, but also the ability to provide better service for the machine — better availability, security, performance and change management.

Better availability means less downtime for the customer; better security means not only ensuring there aren't any viruses, but also notifying the customer when security patches are available for the software on the machine; better performance might mean telling the customer how to better use the machine; and because so much of modern machines is software, better change management means ensuring the customer knows there are new features available merely by upgrading their software. Based on usage data, equipment suppliers can suggest more appropriate models or companion equipment. All of us have seen Amazon provide personal and relevant information regarding other products that we might be interested in, so why not do the same things on the industrial side?

Precision Machines: Reduce cost of service

Traditional computer hardware service requires "rolling a truck" to bring spare parts to repair or service a machine. By connecting the machines, not only could you diagnose problems remotely, but also if you need to make a house call, you could make sure you brought the right part. All of this factors in to dramatically reducing the cost to deliver a service.

These principles are now available to the manufacturers of MRI scanners, locomotives and wind turbines. By connecting these Things to the Internet, manufacturers of machines can reduce their cost of service. First, by being able to diagnose problems remotely, you can dramatically reduce cost. Second, ensuring that required parts are both available and arrive with the service technician reduces repeat visits.

Maintenance of machines — whether that's high-speed inserters, 19-foot scissor lifts or HVACs — is often left as a cost to the purchaser. As consumers who have purchased cars or computers, we know how true that is. These maintenance costs can be significant. A large construction rental company spends more than one billion dollars per year in maintenance. General practice today is to implement time-based maintenance. As a driver, this means that every 12,000 miles you should put oil in your car, no matter if you drive it on a track or to your kids' school. While this is the best we can do in a non-connected world, once we can connect many Things, it becomes possible to know the difference between a forklift that's been used in a sandy, high-humidity, high-temperature environment and one that's been in an air-conditioned warehouse for the past year. Being able to know precisely when the offshore wind turbines need service and being able to do that proactively has significant operational and economic benefit.

Precision Machines: New business models

Manufacturers have traditionally focused on producing a physical good and capturing value by transferring ownership of that good to the customer through a sales transaction. The owner is then responsible for the costs of servicing the product and other costs of use, while assuming the risks of downtime, other product failures and defects not covered by warranties. Smart, connected products allow the radical alteration of this long-standing business model.

Leading machine manufacturers are beginning to understand that the Internet has the potential to change their business models. There are three different business models that will allow for new sources of revenue and create product differentiation.

Luckily, we can learn from our friends in the software industry. Early in the software-product industry we created products and sold them on a CD; if you wanted the next product, you'd have to buy the next CD. As software products became more complex, companies like Oracle moved to a business model where you bought a product license and a support and maintenance contract. That service contract was priced at a derivative of the product purchase price. Over time, this became the largest and most profitable component of many enterprise software product companies.

Next, these companies said if you connect your machines they could offer you advisory services. As the manufacturer of the software product, with knowledge of how it was being used, you could tell the client they could increase the security by applying this software patch, or increase the performance by making changes to the database. Of course, once you can tell the customer how to manage the availability, security, performance and change in the software, it's a simple matter to offer to do it for them.

So, the second generation of enterprise software companies (WebEx, Salesforce, NetSuite, etc.) built their software and processes so they could manage the security, availability, performance and change of the product they manufactured. Service and support levels could be guaranteed because the management of the product was now in the hands of the manufacturer. These business models allowed for customers to purchase the services on-demand and resulted in differentiated and highly valued software-as-a-service companies.

Machine Business Models
The hardware product companies can now leverage this path paved by the software product companies — whether it's a seed drill, chiller or CT scanner — by adding three new business models.

- Service and Support Contracts. Machine sales bundled with warranty or service contracts. Service contracts allow the manufacturer to keep service in-house and capture more of the value from service efficiencies.

- Assisted Services. Connect to the machine and offer advice to improve the availability, security or performance of the machine.

- Machine-as-a-Service. The machine manufacturer retains ownership and takes full responsibility for the security, availability, performance and change of the product in return for a recurring charge. You've seen this for enterprise applications and now for compute and storage computing.

The Internet has enabled the "as-a-service" business model for IT infrastructure and software. The Internet of Things enables "machines-as-a-service" business models for all kinds of other products, potentially letting many kinds of companies shift from selling products to selling services based on those products. This model can transform large capital expenditures into a pay-by-usage operating expense. Examples of this trend are proliferating. They include selling power by the hour, air by the minute, or cubic meters of coal mined. Such services will often be more profitable than the products they are based on. In your industry, you may not want to be the first to do this, but you certainly don't want to be the last.

Precision Service

Some of you who manage hospitals, airlines, farms or factories have heard about the Internet of Things. While many will wonder why a coffee pot needs to communicate with a toaster, there is and will be precision technology, which can dramatically transform the planet's fundamental infrastructure. Later we'll briefly describe the types of technologies which can help build precision machines and more importantly, discuss what the benefits are of using these machines to power precision industries: precision farming, precision power or precision healthcare.

Machine vs. Nomic Data

Before we discuss the benefits of using precision machines, there is an interesting question of who owns what data: machine maker or machine user? Data from agricultural equipment, compressors or gene sequencers will consist of two kinds of data: machine data and what I call *nomic* data. A gene sequencer has machine data such as the power level of the laser or the amount of chemical reagents. While that's machine data, there is also ge-nomic data — the actual gene sequence — also available from the machine. On the farm there are seed spreaders and fertilizer sprayers. Again, there is machine data like speed, oil pressure or location, but also there is also agro-nomic data like the nitrogen level of the soil or the moisture level of the grain. Should all machine data be available to the builders of machines? Large car manufactures might not want to share the data from the robots used to make their cars, as you might be able to forecast the car company's quarterly results. Semiconductor manufacturers might not want sensitive process data outside their four walls. Or Chinese wind turbine companies might not want energy data in a foreign country. This is going to be an ongoing debate, as clearly the machine manufacturer can only build a more reliable, secure, performant product if the data is shared. We're only at the beginning of this debate.

Precision Service: Lower consumables cost

Many machines consume materials during operations. This could be fuel in the case of an airplane, ink for a high-speed printer or chemical reagents in a gene sequencer. Often these consumables form a large portion of the operational cost structure. As anyone with an inkjet printer knows, the cost of the printer is not near as much as the cost of the toner cartridge you buy every year before tax day. At the enterprise level in the airline industry, the single largest operational cost is fuel — in some cases that's nearly 30% of the total cost of the flight.

In the railroad business, New York Air Brake has engineered a product to help operate trains more precisely. This product — LEADER — is being used by Norfolk Southern Railway, which operates over 22,000 route miles in 22 eastern states. They attribute a five percent fuel savings to their deployment of LEADER, resulting in not only 10.8 million gallons of diesel fuel saved per year, but also the avoidance of more than 109,500 metric tons of greenhouse gas emissions.

Leroy Walden at McKenney's engineered a solution to enable more precise power management at Eglin Air Force Base. Covering more than 700 square miles, Eglin is one of the largest military bases in the world and includes 131 buildings. The U.S. Department of Energy's Federal Energy Management Program (FEMP) chose Eglin as the recipient of a 2015 energy and water conservation award. The award recognizes Eglin's innovative approach for combining advanced technologies and common sense to save critical energy resources and reduce utility costs for the base. By integrating direct digital controls, facility sensors and comprehensive energy analytics, the project saved 181 billion BTUs of electricity and natural gas across all the buildings. That's a savings of $3.4M per year.

By connecting machines and learning from them, machine operators can make different decisions about how to use those machines with far lower operational costs.

Precision Service: Higher quality product or service

As the operator of a utility, farm or airline, connecting your machines — your Things — and collecting and learning from the data should also improve the precision of your operations. As an example, consider how precision coal mining machines enable higher output.

Joy Global builds mining machines. One of these is called a longwall system. A longwall system is composed of the shearer, powered-roof-support system, armored face conveyor, belt conveyor, power supply, monorail and pump stations. Massive shearers cut coal from a wall face, which then falls onto a chain conveyor belt for removal. As the longwall advances along the coal seam, the roof behind the roof support's path is allowed to collapse. When a typical system moves forward in the mine, it can extract 2,200 tons of material per hour, which fills a 100-ton railcar in less than one minute.

The longwall system has thousands of sensors. One type is a vibration sensor, which measures vibration on three axes. The data is made available at 10,000Hz — that's 10,000 times per second. Joy Global has developed some sophisticated algorithms that, based on the mining-nomic data, can predict a roof collapse. A roof collapse is very expensive because the debris covers the walkway and the miners have to clear it out. When you realize that will take an average of 7–10 days to dig out the machine and the cost of being offline is $15,000 per minute of downtime, it's clear why you'd like to predict the problem. Based on many data points, including roof support pump pressure, Joy Global can predict a problem. Today, they have longwall mining systems that have not had a roof fault in more than nine months.

Precision Service: Improved health

Precision farming can also lower the cost of consumables (e.g., fuel, fertilizer, pesticides). Nick August is a precision farmer and the owner of August Farms, a family owned business for more than 70 years. Nick grows wheat, rapeseed and peas on 1,235 acres located in the Cotswold just east of London. He estimates that by using precision agricultural machines and a technique referred to as "controlled-traffic farming" and "no-till crop establishment," he can reduce fuel consumption from 60 to 5.9 liters per hectare for crop establishment.

But remember he's also using various fertilizer and pesticides. While reducing the consumption does reduce cost, by reducing chemical usage he's creating a healthier product and doing less damage to the environment.

Precision Service: Improved safety

The derailment of an Amtrak train in Philadelphia in 2015 left at least six people dead and created chaos on the heavily traveled Northeast corridor the next morning, cutting off all direct rail service between Philadelphia and New York City and causing many other delays up and down the east coast. We already talked about how New York Air Brake's assisted services are reducing fuel consumption at Norfolk Southern Railway; this is implemented by providing advice to the train operators on how to operate the train more efficiently. But if you can tell the train operator what to do, it's a short step to just having the computers do it.

In 2016, the first automated train will run from the north of Australia to Perth to deliver iron ore. Not only will it reduce costs, as the railroad spends $300,000 in salary for these operators, but it will also reduce human error, resulting in a safer railroad.

Summary

While technology is cool, its real usage has been to transform businesses. We're all familiar with the examples from the consumer space (Google, Uber, eBay), but IoT technology has the potential to do the same for producers and consumers of the machines used in agriculture, healthcare, power, transportation, water and more. For a manufacturer of Things, technology can not only reduce the cost and improve the quality of service, but also deliver new revenue sources. As a consumer of this next generation of Things, you have the ability to use precision machines to deliver higher quality and lower cost food, power and water, and safer and lower cost transportation and healthcare.

12

Do in Practice

We're still in the very early stages of seeing what IoT technology will do for manufacturers of machines and those who use them. General Electric has done some analysis of a one-percent change in the industries they serve. For instance, as a precision manufacturer of oil and gas machines, an improvement in machine availability by one percent would save nearly $7B per year. As a precision airline or utility, a one-percent savings in fuel across the industry would result in $2–3B in savings per year. Likewise, in the power industry, a one-percent savings in fuel across the industry would add up to nearly $5B in savings annually.

While these are industry wide estimates, we'll explore a few cases that quantitatively or qualitatively illustrate the implications. At the end the chapter, we'll talk about some of the qualities we might see in next-generation IoT applications and middleware.

Precision Machines

Improved Quality of Service

In the wind-turbine business, manufacturers offer turbine operations and maintenance (O&M) services; these services typically range from $20,000 to $50,000 per year for each turbine. Modern large wind turbines are often warranted to run at 95–97% availability, which is achieved partly by the quality of the machine and partly by the quick human response of the O&M team. Imagine the challenges of servicing large, off-shore wind farms and think about the implication of having computers that can predict failure and improve performance based on knowledge from many wind turbines, coupled with current weather and local demand.

Reduced Cost of Service

Pitney Bowes is planning on using data from its high-speed printers and inserters to not only assess performance and problems with onsite technicians, but also engage more senior-level technicians, located in their technology center, to drive down mean time to service. Currently, monitoring the machines takes a large number of personnel physically located near the machine. When problems occur, resolution takes time to diagnose and receive the replacement parts. With IoT applications, cost of service will be reduced.

As a manufacturer of jet engines, GE is using IoT applications to move from time-based to needs-based maintenance. Pulling an engine out for maintenance costs roughly $1M. In 2015, GE eliminated 160 engine pulls by using data and software, which translates into better and lower-cost service.

New Business Models

GE has already shifted significant parts of their business to include service contracts along with the sale of the machine. They've also provided assisted services in some of their business. Their M&D

Center serves more than 500 customer sites providing assisted services to power-plant customers in more than 50 countries.

Some companies have taken the next logical step and have begun to offer machines as a service. One company of note is Kaeser Compressor, which offers air-as-a-service. As another example, one of AGCO's distributors in Brazil offers machines-as-a-service to farms with a guarantee that the farmer gets a minimum of 87% machine uptime without incurring the large upfront cost of purchasing the equipment.

Precision Service Industries

Lower Consumable Cost
As service industries like railroads, utilities and airlines begin to deploy precision machines, they will also derive benefits. Norfolk Southern Railway, with headquarters in Norfolk, Virginia and Atlanta, Georgia, operates more than 22,000 route miles in 22 eastern states. They attribute a 5% fuel savings to their deployment of an IoT application, resulting in 10.8 million gallons of diesel fuel saved and the avoidance of more than 109,500 metric tons of greenhouse gas emissions.

Eglin Air Force Base has deployed an IoT application to provide dashboards to help maintenance staff assess building performance and energy efficiency, generate automated Air Force and DoD energy usage reports, compare current energy usage with historical data and enable the deployment of load shedding and load-shifting strategies to take advantage of favorable electric rates. The application is projected to save about $2.5 million annually in energy costs, with a payback period of less than three years. UK-based Yorkshire Water is measuring chemical usage and, as a result, moved from scheduled delivery to on-demand ordering, eliminating £45,000 in excess chemical costs per year.

Higher Quality Product

Nick August of August Farms might be one of the most technology powered farmers in the world. He's the only one I've met who can explain seed drills, nitrogen levels and RS-232 interfaces. While he's on the leading edge of implementing technology, one of his goals is to create a better agricultural product — one that uses water conservatively and doesn't saturate the land with too many chemical fertilizers or his crops with unnecessary pesticides.

Improved Health and Safety

IoT applications can also reshape the financial services industry. IAAH, a Canadian insurance company, deployed the Mobiliz to connect customers' cars, providing numerous benefits of these new connected services to its customers. First, there is the ability to save money; approximately 80% of customers have been awarded a discount on their insurance premiums for safe-driving behavior. And, best of all, the service can result in higher levels of safety. According to recent analysis, 62% of the "bad" drivers in the Mobiliz program had already improved their driving behavior.

While these are all early stories of the business outcomes of IoT applications, much work remains. As we've said before, Things aren't people, and there will be both new packaged applications and middleware for developers to build custom applications.

Packaged IoP Applications

Just as with the Internet of People, we'll see packaged applications like financials, ERP, CRM and HR applications for the Internet of Things. While there may not be many horizontal applications, one example Thing might be asset-, machine- and device-management. A Thing-management application can be different in significant ways:

- Engineered and delivered as a cloud service. Just hosting traditional asset management applications, like IBM's Maximo, is not the same as engineering them from the ground up to be cloud-based apps. Just compare Siebel to Salesforce or Exchange to Gmail to understand the difference.

- Architected around Things, not people. We've already made the point that Things are not people. Asset-management applications and service-management applications, like ServiceNow, are people-centric, not Thing-centric.

- Architected around smart, connected Things. Last-generation asset management assumed you walked around and inventoried the assets. You had to be physically close. Next-generation Thing-management assumes you can find the Thing (asset, machine, device) on the network — and the network could be cellular, WiFi, ZigBee etc.

- Things are smart. We've had to have people issue trouble tickets, but when there is a 1GHz microprocessor in all our Things, why do we need to do that?

- Connected. Traditional applications are only focused on a single Thing owned and maintained by a company. These are typically deployed on-premise and never engineered to connect to the Internet. For example, you'd never be able to know the re-sale value of your generator, blood analyzer or gene sequencer in the global market — something we can easily do today with any consumer product.

- Engineered for security and privacy. While every application has some authentication and access control, most traditional asset-management and service-management applications never expected the level of threats in the network nor found ways to manage and control them.

Next-Generation Middleware

Custom, industry-specific applications dominated the last generation of enterprise applications (as few applications are truly horizontal). This next generation promises to be no different. If that's the case, we're going to need a middleware layer. While some extension of existing IoP middleware has emerged that supports security, workflow or user-interface design, there will be many reasons why this will be inadequate for IoT applications. As an example, consider:

- Security for IoT applications must be bi-directional. Not only do you need to manage the identity and credentials of Things and their access to the system (protect the system against the Things), you also need to manage the credentials for the system to access each of the Things (protect the Things against the system).

- Machine versus nomic data. AGCO talks about the "two-pipe" approach, but we're going to need to be able to control and secure data about the fertilizer-spraying machine from the agronomic data, or data about the reagents in a blood-analysis machine from blood-analysis results. This has never been true about IoP applications.

- Much of IoP middleware is based on the idea of transaction integrity. In the event of a failure, you roll back the transaction; the physical world runs on the time axis and time does not roll backwards.

- Things won't use UIs. Things only follow concrete procedures defined by their internal mechanics. Such requirements call for a much more sophisticated Thing interaction framework between Things and the application.

We're in the very early stages of this third generation of enterprise software. But you can already see early signs of how software promises to change both the manufacturers of machines and the many industries that use those machines to deliver services the planet depends on.

13

Summary – Principles and Practices

IoT could easily represent the third major generation of enterprise software and hardware technology. You can go to the Internet and find many projections about how big IoT is going to be. Given that the first two generations of enterprise software have basically just automated some back-office functions (HR, payroll, financials) and have left the fundamental businesses untouched, you might agree that IoT may hold the promise to actually transform fundamental businesses.

As in other technology markets, the IoT market will have a variety of players and strategies. Some suppliers will compete by offering distinctive technology, while others will offer distinctive data. Some will try to be platform plays, both through organic investment and acquisitions, and others will still focus on a particular product space. And still, others will offer technology consulting and services to put all of the pieces together.

So the question I raise is why are these IoT products and services not merely an extension of the first and second-generation products? The simple and obvious answer is: Things aren't people. All of the technology we've built to date has been to build IoP applications, not IoT. While all of the stories in this book are using current technology, what is in front of us will look significantly different.

IoT applications differ from IoP applications in three fundamental ways.

- A lot more Things than people. You can't be on the Internet these days and not see some pronouncement about how many things are going to get connected. John Chambers, former CEO of Cisco, recently declared there will be 500 billion Things connected by 2024; that's nearly 100 times the number of people on the planet.

- Things can tell you more than people. The major mechanism people use to tell applications anything is a keyboard, and most applications use some type of form to collect simple amounts of data from individuals. Things have many more sensors; a cell phone has nearly 14 sensors including an accelerometer, GPS and even a radiation detector. Industrial Things like wind turbines, gene sequencers or high-speed inserters can easily have more than 100 sensors.

- Things can talk constantly. Most of the data from IoP applications comes from either encouraging us to buy something or making it part of the hiring process. In short, people don't enter data frequently into an ecommerce, HR, purchasing, CRM or ERP application. On the other hand, a phase measurement unit can send data 60 times per second; a high-speed inserter can send data once every two seconds; and a construction forklift can send data once per minute.

Sensors continue to drop in price and increase in functionality. James Park, founder and CEO of Fitbit, once commented in my Stanford class that we're getting to the point where some devices, formally thought of as only available in the hospital setting, can be brought to a consumer price point. Connection technology has largely been based on people randomly communicating from people-friendly locations. If we have constant communication from many more locations around the planet, what new connection infrastructure could emerge? How will we build communication networks that stream from Things back to the cloud?

Historically, we've collected data in SQL databases. While we've built larger ones, put them in memory, etcetera, we know that the overhead of providing transaction integrity and the ability to equally read and write data is huge. There are already alternatives that are one-tenth the cost to collect the data. Of course, all of this data will be stored and managed as a cloud service, avoiding the cost and unreliability of the handcrafted, on-premise solutions.

Once collected (and we know we can collect a lot more data), our traditional business-intelligence technologies are inadequate. While machine learning has been used in certain applications, there is the opportunity to bring it to a much wider audience. And as we've seen in the last generation, there will need to be middleware that can provide the IoT application programmer with the tools and services to quickly and reliability build applications.

There will be challenges both technically and organizationally — in particular, the increased concern and reality of a hostile world where shutting down the power grid could be as catastrophic as the bombing of Pearl Harbor. As a result, every component of the framework will need to provide security features. Security will need to evolve to be on an equal footing with product features. So what's a security feature?

Hardening a machine means you have all good software and no bad software. If I'm providing a compute and storage cloud service, then this includes all of the software managing and delivering the compute and storage service, as well as all of the software in the datacenter, including power management and building access.

Recognizing this, let's focus on just one aspect: having all good software. Every vendor releases security patches on a regular and (sometimes) emergency basis. In a particular compute and storage cloud service, this could easily translate to hundreds of patches per quarter.

Imagine a cloud service provider saying:

"Within 92 minutes, +/- 5 minutes of the release of all security patches, we perform 1,124 tests and place the patch into production within 22 hours, +/- 10 minutes."

What if a machine provider and could say the same thing?

Technology is built, sold and delivered by people. One of our biggest challenges will be education, both on new technologies and an increasing understanding of the domains of healthcare, mining and water treatment. Today in technology, the world has about ten million programmers, but a back-of-the-envelope analysis says there are probably only ten thousand people who have ever had a basic education in machine learning. With the potential to collect so much data, we'll have to meet the challenge of educating a new generation. It won't just be education on connection, collection or learning technology — it's also going to be education on the domains. In the past year, I have learned an amazing amount about farming, high-speed printing and gene sequencers. We're going to need to find a way to have our technologists understand more about the domains, and for domain experts to be able to speak the language of the technologists.

While there are many more challenges — seen and unseen — this area remains one where the opportunity for innovation is high and the impact on both the planet and people's lives might be much greater than we've seen so far. We will need more precision technology to build precision machines for the sake of providing precision services to the world.

Book 2: Solutions

14

Introduction – Solutions

The first book described the fundamental technologies required to build Internet of Things (IoT) applications. This book takes the point of view of the manufacturer of precision machines and the services that use those machines to provide precision services. It is organized as a series of cases designed to be read by technologists and business people. The cases describe the solutions' various technology components and the business value to the customers. Furthermore, they will be as specific as possible but invite the reader to learn more about any particular technology.

You'll also see that some cases are from the point of view of the manufacturer (e.g., high speed inserter, gene sequencer or locomotive), and some from the point of view of the service company (e.g., hospital, rail line or utility) that uses the machines to provide a precision service. For example, you'll see the AGCO case, which is a manufacturer of agricultural machines, as well as the August Farms case, a farm that uses AGCO equipment and many other kinds of machines. For all cases we'll use the framework of Things, Connect, Collect, Learn and Do.

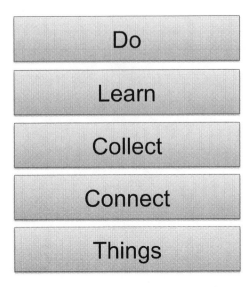

Figure 14.1 IoT Framework

Things

Whether a train operator like Norfolk Southern or an equipment provider to that operator like New York Air Brake, the section called *Things* will describe what the Thing is and what kind of data is being sensed. We'll show you specific examples wherever possible and describe the hardware and software environment and how it's being secured on a particular Thing, whether it's an air conditioner or a high-speed printer.

Connect

This section describes how the machines are connected. We'll discuss both the network layer (cellular, WiFi, ZigBee etc.) as well as the application layer (HTTP, MQTT etc.). Some cases will also discuss how the connection is secured between the Thing and the cloud.

Collect

Once connected, there are various ways the data can be collected, ranging from SQL and time-series databases to noSQL implementations. This section discusses the technology being used, how much data is being stored, and decisions around frequency and duration of archiving or retention.

Learn

Everyone is trying analyze and learn from data, whether that's driving patterns, energy usage or human vital signs. Each of the cases will cover what technology is being used to analyze the data.

Do

Finally, what should you do with what you've learned? We'll discuss both autonomous and semi-autonomous operation, but more importantly, the *Do* section will describe the business benefit — whether that's to the manufacturer or the user of the Thing. For several cases we'll also describe the business outcome in financial terms.

There is a subtle — or not so subtle — difference between the types of data coming from machines. AGCO calls this a "two-pipe" approach; we'll make it more generic and point out that there is both machine information and what we will call *nomic* information. For example, a gene sequencer may have sensor information describing the reagent or voltage level of the machine (machine information) but also deliver genomic information — your DNA sequence. We make this distinction because there is much debate about who owns the information: the company that builds the machine, the company that rents or maintains the machine or the company that uses the machine.

Companies that build the machines are called Original Equipment Manufacturers (OEMs) and they want access to the machine data to improve the quality and reduce the cost of service of the machines. As noted, they make a distinction between nomic and machine data and, as we'll see in later chapters, provide two different access methods.

Companies that rent or service machines, which are often the sales and service channel for OEMs, don't want the OEMs to have access to even the machine information and have taken steps to disable the OEMs devices and instead put their own device on the machines. This is because in addition to the equipment-status information, the same device will give the OEM access to information about where and how it is being used. In some industries, OEMs regularly try to get into the rental business and compete.

It obviously makes no sense to have two separate systems for the machine data. The channel also realizes there is a benefit from the OEM learning about the performance of their machine so they can improve them. Just as we've seen on the consumer side, the question of data ownership is far from resolved, so stay tuned.

As the reader, you may choose to only read the chapters about your specific industry, but our hope is that you'll read across industries, as there are many different approaches to applying these technologies to build IoT applications. We've taken the approach that everyone is a novice in some industry, so you'll see the appropriate amount of background and a limited use of acronyms; so whether you're in oil and gas or mining, you'll be able to understand the agriculture or healthcare cases.

15

Precision Mailing

Pitney Bowes Inc. provides postage, printing, mailing and shipping technology products and solutions internationally. The company operates through small and medium business solutions, enterprise business solutions and digital commerce solutions segments. In 2013, Roger Pilc joined Pitney Bowes as CIO to accelerate its digital transformation. This case will focus on his team's work in enterprise business solutions, which offers equipment and services to enable large enterprises to create large-scale mailings including bills and statements.

With the emergence of new digital channels, mail volume has declined; however, large-volume mailers like banks or insurance companies continue to use physical mail for their most important direct communications. For the purpose of this discussion, think of high-volume mail as a manufactured product produced on enterprise-class equipment. The manufacturing process involves three major steps: print, insert and sort.

Things

The industrial-strength machines used by Pitney Bowes are just like any other manufacturing equipment — a combination of mechanics, electronics, consumables and software. Sensors throughout the machines control the process and detect faults. All mail manufacturing factories operate on defined service level agreement (SLA) requirements; therefore, the health and availability of equipment is critical to their success. To this end, major mailers invest in service contracts and spare parts inventories.

Manufacturing mail starts with high-volume printing. Pitney Bowes provides both the AcceleJet and IntelliJet high-volume printing systems. These systems can generate 4–10 million direct mail printing impressions per month. These high-volume printers can provide information including job status, dryer temperature and ink-jet head/nozzle status.

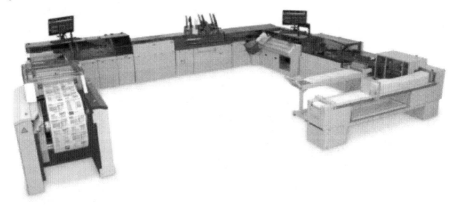

Figure 15.1 Pitney Bowes Epic Inserter

After printing, the mail needs to be inserted into envelopes. Pitney Bowes builds a high-volume inserter — the Epic Inserter, shown in Figure 15.1 — which can stuff envelopes at the rate of 22,000 pieces per hour while also allowing quick changeovers to different envelope types.

The inserters are controlled by dozens of servomotors and have hundreds of sensors to monitor the flow of mail and provide feedback to the control system. Specifically, some of these sensors provide information on:

- Motor RPM
- Motor-shaft position
- Velocity of mail material (sheets, envelopes, mail pieces)
- Position of mail material
- Skew of mail material
- Material thickness and weight
- Air pressure
- Vacuum levels where air is used to control the machine

The sensors are all attached to local compute and storage, which are one or more industrial PCs mounted inside the machine and networked together to share data and synchronize control of the machine. These PCs are running Microsoft Windows with a real-time extension, called RTX from IntervalZero, to provide the deterministic response required for machine control. For security purposes, antivirus software is also running.

Connect

Pitney Bowes connects the inserters to the Internet through a Cisco 819 Integrated Services Router. One Cisco device per mail manufacturing site is used and placed on the network segment for the customer's fleet of inserters.

The Cisco 819 Integrated Services Router is the smallest Cisco IOS software router with support for integrated wireless WAN and LAN capabilities. The Cisco 819 also has a virtual machine and supports the execution of software developed by Pitney Bowes. Every five minutes, this software checks the contents of the sensor-data files, which are continuously accumulating, prior to pushing the data to GE's Predix platform. This validation check ensures that no Personally Identifiable Information (PII) is transmitted. Log files are created that allow Pitney Bowes and its clients to view and block content.

Data is transferred via a secure, Transport Layer Security (TLS) connection. TLS and its predecessor, Secure Sockets Layer (SSL), (both of which are frequently referred to as "SSL") are cryptographic protocols designed to provide communication security over a network. Several versions of the protocols are in widespread use in applications such as web browsing, email, Internet faxing, instant messaging and voice over IP (VoIP). Major websites including Google, YouTube and Facebook use TLS to secure all communications between their servers and web browsers. At the end of 2015, Pitney Bowes had two sites with multiple inserters connected and they expect to have more than one hundred connected by the end of 2016.

Collect

Pitney Bowes is using GE's Predix as a platform for a series of new IoT applications. Predix itself is composed of various types of micro services including machine, asset, security, analytic, connectivity and data services.

- *Machine services.* A device-independent software stack to develop solutions to securely connect machines to the Industrial Internet and perform edge analytics.

- *Asset services.* Enables application developers to create and store assets that define asset properties as well as relationships between assets and other modeling elements.

- *Security services*. Manage application tenants, provide user authentication and add granular authorization mechanisms to access services without having to add complex authorization code.

- *Connectivity services*. Provide connections — either wirelessly or over the Internet — from their machines to Predix. These are the higher level services we discussed in the *Connect Principles* chapter of the first book.

- *Data services*. Ability to ingest, store and analyze time-series and operational data.

Pitney Bowes controls the rate at which data is pushed. For the first two applications — dubbed *Clarity Advisor* and *Clarity Optimizer* — data will be pushed three times a day. For the third application, they will push to the cloud every five minutes. The data is live in GE's Predix for at least two years before its archived and collected in a SQL database within Predix.

Learn

Pitney Bowes uses GE's analytics services, which provide a framework for developing and embedding advanced analyses. The framework can be used to manage the execution of analytics through configuration, abstraction and extensible modules.

The *Clarity Advisor* IoT application is focused on improving uptime. Three key metrics are monitored: machine efficiency, operator efficiency and bad out sorts. Each of these is expressed as a percentage, with the ideal being one hundred percent machine and operator efficiency and zero percent bad out sorts. Machine efficiency takes processing speed and outages into account. Operator efficiency is a measurement of how attentive the operator is to the process. For example, do they let the machine run out of raw materials? Are they effective in clearing paper jams in a normal (for the industry) period of time? The last metric, out sort percentage, is equivalent to yield. Out sorted pieces indicate defective pieces or pieces that need QA.

Whenever the machine stops due to an error, an error code is recorded. A single error by itself is not necessarily an indication of equipment failure, but by analyzing trends of errors under various conditions, it is possible to identify the components that are beginning to fail and should be replaced. Error trends can be observed per machine and broken down further to a combination of machine and specific operator or machine and specific job. The error trends can be further analyzed by going one level deeper to a combination of machine, specific operator and specific job.

Do

Pitney Bowes uses GE's Predix Asset service to create and store assets and define asset properties and relationships between assets. Within Predix, each Pitney inserter is an asset with various attributes such as customer name, machine name, model, serial number, etc.

Improve Quality of Service
As a machine manufacturer, Pitney Bowes will be using what they learn from the inserters to concurrently assess performance and problems with both onsite technicians and more senior-level technicians to drive down mean time to service, thereby increasing quality of service to their customers.

Quality of service should also be improved due to the analytic software continuously monitoring every inserter and issuing alerts to service personnel to address specific machine components before their failure disrupts production.

Reduce Cost of Service

Currently, monitoring the machines take a large number of personnel physically located near the machine. When problems occur, resolution takes time to both diagnose and receive the replacement parts. With this software, cost of service should be reduced due to centralization of the monitoring and more effective dispatching of service personnel with the correct parts the first time. This can result in either decreased cost of service contracts to the customer or increased margin to Pitney Bowes.

Improve Productivity

As for Pitney Bowes' customers, one of the central benefits is improved productivity, which reduces the cost per mail piece. Productivity is highly dependent upon the right mix of machine, operator and job attributes; so Pitney Bowes has created benchmarks that compare the performance of each job to the performance of all like jobs in the database at a particular site. Furthermore, they can also benchmark across the entire customer base to highlight other productivity improvement opportunities. Who knows, one day they may offer printers and inserters as a service.

16

Precision Trains

Be prepared to have a high-tech discussion when talking to Greg Hrebek, the director of engineering at New York Air Brake (NYAB). His LinkedIn profile describes him as a "transformational artist specializing in global customers and emerging technologies." NYAB is a division of Knorr-Bremse, a multi-billion-dollar firm based in Germany, and has been a leading supplier to the railroad industry of braking systems and components, training simulators and train control systems for 125 years.

Beginning with its train-simulator business, NYAB has been increasingly using information from Things to improve operational efficiency. This will culminate next year in the first autonomous freight train running in Australia as part of Rio Tinto's *Mine of the Future* initiative, which also includes driverless trucks and autonomous drills. On its 1,500-kilometer rail network, Rio Tinto currently runs 41 trains from mines to ports, comprising 148 locomotives and 9,400 iron ore cars. Today, Rio Tinto pays operators upwards of $300,000 per year and flies them into remote locations just to drive the trains, so it's not hard to understand why they're going to autonomous trains.

NYAB's LEADER application is integrated with the locomotive's on-board electronics to provide locomotive engineers with real-time information and assistance via an in-cab display, among many other capabilities.

Things

NYAB deploys on three hardware platforms. The first platform, developed for the U.S. Class 1 market, is the positive train control (PTC) equipment provided by Wabtec. Wabtec collects the sensor data and provides that to NYAB software, running on Wabtec hardware.

The second platform is for Electro-Motive Diesel (EMD) locomotives. In this case, NYAB software runs on a computer made by DEUTA-WERKE and interacts directly with the locomotive systems to leverage existing sensors rather than adding their own.

The final configuration, the Quad-C, is used for international and U.S. short-line railroads. The Quad-C is NYAB's packaging of the National Instruments CompactRIO with a QNX system. In this case, NYAB provides all the sensors and does all the data aggregation. The CompactRIO system runs on a Xilinx ARM architecture system-on-a-chip (SoC). On the software side it runs a special, real-time Linux OS developed by National Instruments. One of the big challenges National Instruments faces in creating platforms for enterprise IoT is getting advanced chipsets from suppliers like Xilinx or Intel to run at higher temperatures without fan cooling. Given the length of time some of these trains are in service, the parts must be made available for ten or more years.

The types of sensor data available include:

- Brake cylinder PSI: The amount of pressure applied to the locomotive's brake cylinders.
- Brake pipe PSI: The current PSI of the locomotive's brake pipe. Compressed air is transmitted along the train to brake each of the cars.
- Equalizing reservoir PSI: A small reservoir used on locomotives to regulate the brake pipe.
- Brake pipe airflow: A flow meter provides air mass flow rate into the brake pipe.
- Current and voltage to traction motors
- Speed
- Engine RPMs
- Location

Sensors will typically record data once per second, although some data is sampled at five times per second. NYAB has more than 4,000 LEADER systems deployed in the field.

Connect

Most locomotives have a Communication Management Unit (CMU) that manages and optimizes routes for data traffic. The CMU contains a variety of data modems including WiFi, cellular and satellite. It may even contain multiple network providers for cellular and satellite; for example, in the U.S. you will see both Verizon and AT&T as cellular providers. The CMU looks at the priority of the data and the cost of transmission and determines the best physical/data-link layer method to use. The CMU also creates a VPN connection with the railroad's back-office-network system so that all traffic is communicated across their private WAN. In addition, SSH is the primary transport layer providing an additional security measure and is required for railroads that don't have the IT infrastructure to utilize the VPN solution.

GE produces the LOCOCOMM, a CMU applicable to both GE and non-GE locomotives. It uses an Intel, single-board computer (256MB DRAM, 512MB Flash expandable to 4GB) with an embedded Microsoft Windows NT operating system. The system operates in any orientation with no external cooling, houses the power supply for the rooftop-antenna package and is powered directly by a 74-volt locomotive battery. In addition to communications, the CMU contains an integrated GPS provisioned for Differential Global Positioning System (an enhancement to GPS), which provides improved location accuracy from the nominal 15-meter GPS accuracy to about 10cm in the best implementations. Strategies for usage will include satellite for small amounts of time-sensitive data to larger files being transferred over WiFi when the train reaches its destination. NYAB will pull information from the train every five minutes in a compressed format. On average, a locomotive supplies 20MB of compressed data per month.

Collect

Train data is transmitted to NYAB's cloud where they use the same detailed physics models running onboard the locomotive to expand the compressed data to a time-series database; this amounts to roughly 40TB per month, per locomotive, 90% of which is time-series data. Interestingly, the physics models sit as the core of their training simulator and are accurate to within one percent of the real world. The models are so precise that NYAB is used by the Federal Railroad Administration (FRA) to do accident investigations.

To process the data, NYAB uses Splunk, which provides real-time and historical search, as well as reports and statistical analysis.

The product can index structured or unstructured, textual, machine-generated data. Search and analytics operations are specified using Search Processing Language. Originally based on Unix Piping and SQL, Splunk's scope includes data searching, filtering, modification, manipulation, insertion and deletion.

NYAB can run a query to retrieve all of the data for a particular trip or set of trips for a set of trains or a single train. Splunk maintains the archive and when they want to analyze the data, it's decompressed on demand and a large CSV file is generated, which is uploaded to bulk storage on Amazon's S3.

Learn

Prior to deploying Splunk, the NYAB team used Excel spreadsheets to prepare monthly reports for customers on system performance and resource utilization. For example, a report might show a customer's fuel savings when they were say 70% compliant with optimal driving recommendations; however, if the customer requested another type of report, it would take another four or five hours to prepare it.

Today, when the data is uncompressed, NYAB does several things with it. The first is to compare the actual train operation to the idealized computer-generated plan. This can be used to monitor driver compliance and assist the train operator in how to reduce in-train forces, reduce fuel spend and improve time-to-destination.

The uncompressed data can also be used to monitor the health of the locomotive. As an example, the horsepower rating of the locomotive will degrade over time. This is a cliff function, so you don't want to hit what they call the *negative impact zone*. So rather than wait for maintenance every 90–180 days, customers can now move to condition-based maintenance and catch a problem much earlier.

NYAB uses both supervised and unsupervised machine learning (ML). As an example, unsupervised ML is used to implement train-handling risk mitigation. They feed the location and the magnitude of the in-train forces along a route, as well as the detailed consist data (length, weight and weight distribution) into ML algorithms and build a model that's used to predict the likelihood of a future train experiencing the same train-handling issues. They can then take an action to issue a slow-speed restriction over a section of track that has a high predicted-risk score to help mitigate that risk.

Supervised ML is used for fuel-efficiency analysis. Based on the analysis of the uncompressed data, they create a data model for fuel consumption based on aspects of train operation excluding train handling. Aspects like wind data, train length, number of stops required and efficiency of the locomotives are used as inputs into multivariable regressions. A time window is created based on seasonal changes in order to keep the data model current. The model's effectiveness is used to determine potential for energy reduction of segments based on the R^2 value. Fuel predictions from the model are used as the baseline where new data is compared to quantify fuel savings. This allows NYAB to predict what is split between environmental aspects of fuel usage and what is in the control of the driver (computer or human).

Of course, NYAB also uses data to implement predictive and prescriptive analytical analysis of brake shoe wear. They can recreate train runs in simulation and very accurately determine how much energy was absorbed by the brake shoes on individual cars. This can then be compared to data models relating brake-shoe wear to the energy absorbed. Given the historical data of the car and the projected route, combined with historical simulation data of that route, NYAB can predict how much wear a brake shoe will experience in future travels.

Do

With headquarters in Atlanta, Georgia and Norfolk, Virginia, Norfolk Southern operates over 22,000 route miles in 22 eastern states. They attribute a 5% fuel savings to their deployment of LEADER, resulting in 10.8 million gallons of diesel fuel saved and the avoidance of more than 109,500 metric tons of greenhouse gas emissions. LEADER not only decreases the cost of maintenance by reducing coupler fatigue, wheel wear and brake-shoe wear, but it also dramatically increases throughput, particularly when integrated with a dispatch planner.

Of course, once you can assist the drivers to optimize time, fuel or reliability, it's not too difficult to imagine turning over the controls to the computer (with the driver along for the ride) to finally moving to fully autonomous operation, like we'll soon see in Australia. Perhaps this will also result in improved safety.

We'll end on a slightly amusing note. Many trains today have a switch that must be pressed every ten minutes to make sure the operator is still alert, but some people have seen operators hit the button even when fully asleep. So train operation may become both lower cost and much safer in the future.

17

Precision Mining

With roots dating back to 1884, Joy Global is a leading producer of mining systems, equipment, parts and services for underground and surface mining of coal, copper, iron ore, oil sands, gold and other mineral resources. Joy Global's machines — longwall systems, continuous miners, haulage systems, conveyors, shovels, loaders and drills — cut, crush, and convey minerals from the mine.

The cost of producing energy and extracting minerals continues to rise as high-grade ores become increasingly scarce and the primary sources of new reserves shift to ever riskier and more remote regions. At the same time, commodity prices have been declining, squeezing profit margins and resulting in a sharp cyclical downturn in mining equipment sales. Mine operators have pushed utilization rates for mining equipment to new highs, averaging 85% for key machinery. However, overall productivity of the mining operation often still lags well behind its potential. Our focus in this case is going to be on coal mining, which has a different set of requirements than surface mining (e.g., iron ore mining). About six billion tons of coal is mined annually, with China producing around four billion tons, the U.S. producing one billion, and the rest of world producing the other one billion. India has the second largest coal reserves in the world. Forty percent of the world's electricity is generated by coal.

Things

Longwall mining is a highly productive underground coal-mining technique. Longwall mining machines consist of a coal shearer and a track-mounted armored face conveyor coupled to a series of self-advancing hydraulic roof supports; the whole process is mechanized. The capital cost required to purchase a longwall machine varies from $45–250M, depending on machine size and complexity. A complete longwall machine weighs close to 15,000 tons, equivalent to 761 John Deere 9560R tractors, and can be up to 1,500-feet wide (five football fields). When I kept referring to these as "machines," Ben Snyman at Joy Global reiterated that it's much more than a machine given its size and complexity, referring to it rather as a longwall *system*.

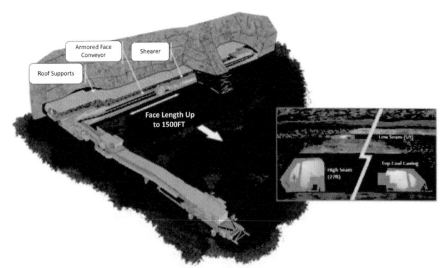

Figure 17.1 Longwall System

A longwall system is composed of the shearer, powered-roof-support system, armored face conveyor, belt conveyor, power supply, monorail and pump stations. Figure 17.1 gives you some sense of how it works. Massive shearers cut coal from a mine wall containing a coal seam (face), and the coal falls onto a chain conveyor belt for removal. As the longwall shearer advances along the coal seam, the roof supports automatically move forward and the roof behind the roof supports' path is allowed to collapse. A typical longwall system can extract 2,200 tons of material per hour, and fill a 100-ton railcar in less than one minute.

One of Joy Global's biggest machines has a shearing drum that is four meters in diameter. These longwall systems utilize 7,000 sensors to monitor and control system performance. Data is transferred between individual pieces of equipment and up to the surface.

Although the longwall shearer is relatively small compared to the entire system, it is controlled by complex algorithms that onboard the machine. Shearers can have six onboard motors, 12 hydraulic functions, military grade inertial navigation sensor, color and infrared cameras, and a radio control interface; they also utilize high accuracy incremental encoders to measure movement. The shearer takes real-time measurements of a multitude of temperatures, oil levels, vibrations, pressure and flows. Due to the flameproof/explosion-proof requirements for equipment used in underground coalmines, most of the instrumentation is custom-engineered.

On board the shearer is a Consolidated Controller Unit (CCU). The latest generation CCU uses a 1.6GHz Intel microprocessor with 2GB of memory running Wind River's VxWorks, a real-time operating system. The CCU monitors and controls the movement of the shearing arms to accuracies of within two inches. Together, with input from the machine and operators, the CCU monitors and adjusts the powered roof support push increment within fractions of an inch across the face width. To achieve the most stable roof conditions, the roof supports, which advance forward in increments of three feet, need to advance in a near straight line across the entire coal face, which can be up to 1,500 feet long.

Some of the parameters being measured are:

- Motor current — can range from 15 to 700 Amps
- Speed of the shearer — up to 60 feet/minute
- Water flow — water is used for cooling, ignition suppression and dust control, and can flow at up to 280 gallons per minute
- Hydraulic pressure — the pressure applied to the roof supports — up to 350Bar
- Ranging arm height — determines how much of the coal seam can be reached by the shearer — up to 320 inches
- Machine voltage — measures the supply of voltage to the longwall system up to 10,000 volts
- Vibration velocity — measures the instantaneous vibration of the machine parts in millimeters per second
- Temperatures of motors, fluids etc. — monitored in Fahrenheit
- Control voltage — measures voltages in the control circuit, which can be 12, 24 or 110 volts
- Methane — measures methane levels mixed with oxygen as a percentage
- Frequency — measures line frequency of variable speed drives in hertz
- Position of hydraulic cylinder movement — measured in inches
- Inertial navigation system — as six degrees of freedom over time
- Inclinometers — equipment sub-system angle of operation measured in degrees

Connect

Joy Global connects equipment throughout the mine to computers located on the surface using fiber optic and copper data cables, as well as network switches, routers and other computer hardware. They also have a proprietary wireless system that is used for close proximity data transmission underground. As part of the overall architecture, Joy Global has implemented a data concentrator, which allows up to 7,000 data points to be collected at a rate of over 4MB per second in the Joy Global data center.

The wireless system is used underground only on the longwall system to allow for close proximity (200 feet) data transmission. The wireless network uses custom-engineered 2.4GHz WiFi radios that are compatible with 802.11b/g. All data flows are on the dedicated control network, with no other equipment allowed on this dedicated control network. The network is set up and tested to ensure specific latency delays between devices when the longwall is operational. Because it is critical that data is not lost, standard industrial heartbeat and watchdog timers are used. For longer distances, fiber optic and power line modem communication systems are used.

At the end of 2015, 165 machines had been connected to computers on the mine surface. The plan is to add 130 machines in 2016, with the objective of one day connecting all of the more than 5,000 Joy Global machines in the field.

Collect

Data from the longwall machines is collected in AspenTech's InfoPlus.21 (IP21), which is a time-series database, sometimes also referred to as a process historian. In general, data is collected once per second, although there is the potential to transmit 20 and 100 times per second. Data is kept for a year and then archived. Currently some of the systems have seven years' worth of sensor data.

One of the challenges is that data is collected in more than 11 different time zones from equipment on multiple control platforms. All this data needs to be stored and analyzed with respect to the correct time and aligned with asynchronous alarms that get generated, collected and merged again in the Joy Global data center. The company's dedicated JoySmart Solutions experts oversee the analysis of all this data and use global benchmarking to improve performance.

Joy Global found that due to the uniqueness of each underground mine operation and its machines, many technologies needed to be incorporated into the solution, including Honeywell's asset manager, Microsoft's Azure, Verizon's managed hosting, Matrikon's desktop historian and PTC's ThingWorx.

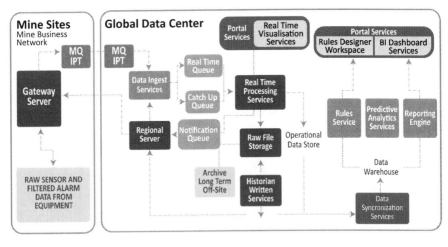

Figure 17.2 IoT Application Architecture

Learn

Two of the key technologies Joy Global uses for shearer lifecycle management are oil analysis and vibration analysis. When the shearer is first built, a blueprint is stored in the data historian. During operation, and at the specified maintenance and repair intervals, sensor data is collected, compared and analyzed for deviation from the norm. Condition-monitoring data is also integrated with the real-time data points collected from the underground machine for the purpose of early identification and warning of potential catastrophic failures.

About 35 parameters are measured for oil analysis; these parameters include the number of parts per million (ppm) of wear metals, contaminant metals, multi-source metals and additive metals. Analyzing oil can help indicate when to change it, as opposed to the every-3,000-miles-method (changing the oil whether you need it or not). Also, being able to see the types of metals in the oil can indicate if a gearbox or bearing is failing; or if water is seen in the oil, then the water jacket is probably failing.

The analytics engine uses data from historical failures and theoretical predictions made by the Joy Global team of statistical analysts. Statistical techniques, such as principal-component analysis, are used to determine correlation between 10–20 variables for early warning and failure predictions. K-Means clustering, linear and multiple regression modeling methods are also used commonly for data exploration and research.

Onboard-vibration analysis allows early intervention when the signature deviates from the norm. Data is collected and stored in the Joy Global data center and analyzed and compared to other machine signatures to ensure that a false warning is not generated. Machines can contain up to 16 vibration-analysis sensors, which measure vibration on three axes. What's amazing is that the data is made available at 10,000Hz — that's 10,000 times per second. Joy Global has developed some sophisticated algorithms that can potentially identify which gear in the machine may be problematic. This technique has also been used for predictive analytics for jet engines.

While learning from machine data is valuable, there is also the ability to learn from nomic data. I suppose we could call it mining-nomic data. One of the most interesting applications is using data from the mine to predict roof collapse. Roof collapse presents an obvious risk to the health and safety of mine personnel as well as a risk of damage to mining equipment. At a minimum, when the roof falls, it covers the walkway and the miners have to clear all of the debris. When you realize that will take an average of 7–10 days to clear the debris, and the cost of being offline is measured at $15,000 per *minute* of downtime, it's clear why you'd like to predict the problem. Based on many data points, including roof support pump pressure, Joy Global can predict a problem and customize a solution through its JoySmart Solutions offering. Today, there are longwall mining systems using Joy Global monitoring and analysis that have not had a roof fault in over nine months.

Do

A longwall system only needs about eight people to operate it, but it takes several hundred people to maintain the system. In fact, the machine requires a daily four-hour maintenance session.

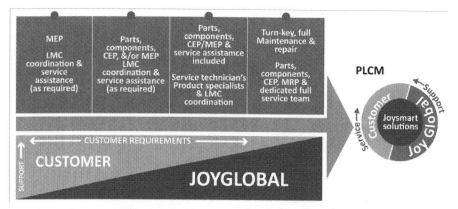

Figure 17.3 Joy Global Services[3]

As a result, Joy Global provides a series of services that range from classic service contracts and assisted services all the way to mining equipment-as-a-service. In Figure 17.3, you can see the range of services, which are identical to what we've seen in the software industry, where at one end we ask the customer to provide the service of the software all the way to delivering software-as-a-service. JoySmart Solutions are Joy Global's top-tier service packages. They are integrations of the company's smart connected products and systems, advanced analytics and direct services customized to solve customers' toughest challenges.

Joy prices these services based on a dollar-per-ton-mined metric. Being able to use data from machines operating across its global network allows JoySmart Solutions experts to provide even more guidance. In one example, a customer mine was running at less than 50% utilization at the processing plant (less than 50 hours of production per week). By eliminating waste and simplifying and automating the process, JoySmart Solutions experts helped increase mine production by 65% and helped increase utilization by 20%, ultimately resulting in more than $100M in additional revenue for the customer's operation.

---

[3] MEP – Machine Exchange Program; LCM – Lifecycle Management; CEP – Component Exchange Program

Most of the company's service packages make the business-model assumption that the mining company purchases the machine upfront. However, for a few customers, Joy Global has made the complete move to providing mining equipment-as-a-service, priced at a higher dollar-per-ton rate. It will be interesting to see what lies ahead.

18

Precision Gene Sequencers

A few years back, I was finally able to schedule Jay Flatley, CEO of Illumina, to be a guest lecturer in my Stanford class. Illumina is the market leader in gene sequencers and has a valuation today that would rival many software companies.

A gene or DNA sequencer is an instrument used to determine the sequence or order of the four bases — G (guanine), C (cytosine), A (adenine) and T (thymine) — from any plant or animal cell. Sequencers works by having a chemical reagent called fluorochromes mixed with the sample. Using lasers, light reflected from the samples yields the sequence information. There are a variety of techniques used to create higher-volume and lower-cost sequencing. Ten years ago, a whole human sequence cost approximately $10M. As you can see in Figure 18.1, over the first decade of gene sequencing, the cost to sequence has been driven down faster than the classic Moore's Law, which has driven the semiconductor and computing industry.

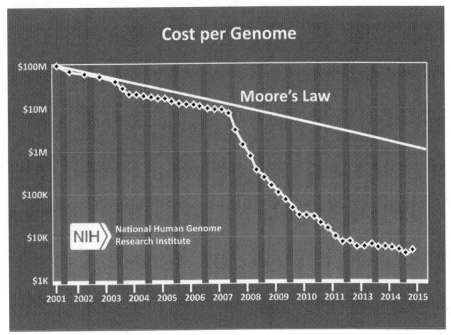

Figure 18.1 Gene Sequencing Costs

Today, the cost of a sequence is approaching $1,000 and a technology roadmap exists to further drive the cost down. While this is an oversimplified explanation, the implications of this technology are just being realized. For example, Jay showed my Stanford class a scan of a patient who was undergoing chemotherapy. The scan showed that the tumor was disappearing, so the chemotherapy was stopped; however, the patient sadly died a few weeks later. He then showed the results of multiple sequences of the patient and you could see that the number of his cancerous cells, which had begun to transform, was indeed increasing. At thousands of dollars per sequence, this can be cost prohibitive; but if this cost was reduced to $100 per sequence, cancer treatment might be changed significantly.

While many of the use cases to date have largely been in the domain of research labs, there are some consumer applications. One example is prenatal DNA testing. Classically, older mothers who are more at risk for having children with genetic abnormalities (like

Down syndrome) are recommended to undergo a procedure called amniocentesis. This is a procedure where a needle is inserted into the mother's womb and amniotic fluid is withdrawn and sent to a lab for testing. The procedure, while routine, can have complications including miscarriages and infections. Illumina has a new product that only requires a blood sample from the mother, which is far less invasive. Surprisingly, the baby's genetic material can be found in the mother's blood sample, which can be sequenced, resulting in the same analysis with none of the risks of amniocentesis.

Things

Some have compared the complexity of a gene sequencer to that of a jet engine. For this case, we'll focus on the Illumina MiniSeq DNA sequencing system, which retails for around $50,000.

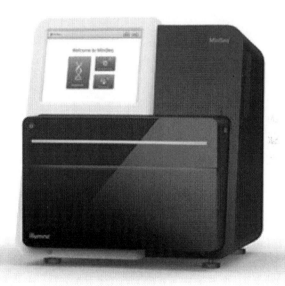

Figure 18.2 Illumina MiniSeq

As the MiniSeq is built with many subcomponents that often have embedded sensors, the true count of the number of sensors is unknown. Nevertheless, the 40 sensors Illumina does record include:

- 1 CCD camera
- 2 RFID readers, 2 sensors each
- 1 photodiode
- 5 motor encoders
- 1 valve position sensor
- 6 fan-speed sensors
- 6 temperature probes
- 1 fluidic pressure sensor
- 15 digital-state sensors

A sample of this type of data is shown in Figure 18.3. The format is a time stamp followed by a key-value pair, where NonRun denotes data collected periodically versus during a sequencing run.

27T17:45:51.1975426Z,ImagingModule.Camera1,ZmotorHeightError,84.5835545959806,D,NonRun,
2016-01-27T17:46:13.8215426Z,Motor.FlowcellX,PositionError,10.7496585746993,D,NonRun,
2016-01-27T17:45:58.9745426Z,Fan.Exhaust0,FanSpeed,43.11476,F,NonRun,
2016-01-27T17:46:01.8025426Z,TempProbe.ThermoCoupleRear,TempRead,8.184425,F,NonRun,
2016-01-27T17:46:02.5095426Z,TempProbe.Camera1,TempRead,66.1964,F,NonRun,
2016-01-27T17:46:17.3565426Z,Fluidics.PressureSensor,Pressure,65.55073,F,NonRun,
2016-01-27T17:46:20.8915426Z,Sensor.FlowCellHomeY,SensorState,T,B,NonRun,
2016-01-27T17:46:21.5985426Z,Sensor.FlowCellClamp,SensorState,F,B,NonRun,

Figure 18.3 Illumina Sensor Data Example

Additionally, there are 229 discrete metrics logged. The vast majority are not time-series, sensor data, but include:

- Subcomponent version numbers, serial numbers, MFR dates and build lots
- Static configuration values such as calibration constants
- Elapsed operating and idle time
- User-entered parameters
- User mouse and keyboard activity

- Operational values sent to sub-components when they are activated (motor move distance, camera exposure etc.)
- Calculated bioinformatic quality metrics of the end-user's output data
- Errors and warnings

The compute and storage environment on the gene sequencer is composed of a 32-bit ARM CPU with 500MB of memory and 2GB of flash storage, along with an FPGA chip with in-house custom logic. This computer runs ThreadX, a real-time operating system from Express Logic. In addition, there is an Intel single-board computer with 16GB of memory and 1TB storage running Windows 7. Software upgrades are downloaded from the cloud and the client chooses when to activate the upgrade.

Connect

Illumina's gene sequencers were engineered to connect to the Internet and the Illumina cloud with Ethernet and a conventional TCP/IP stack running on the Intel single-board computer. Data is transferred with RESTful services over HTTP from the machines. There is the option for customers to use their own intranet for genomic data transfers in order to isolate the machine from the network; for these customers, Illumina's field support staff will periodically access the machines on-premises and copy machine information.

The Advanced Encryption Standard (more advanced than DES) is used to encrypt both machine and genomic data as it's written to local storage. Data in flight to the cloud is secured with OAuth v1.0 authentication and classic SSL transport encryption.

Collect

Data starts out as flat file on the sequencer, uploaded to the cloud as flat files — some encrypted and some as binary files. Some of the data is periodic and some is run-based. These flat files are all stored in Amazon's S3 storage service. Genomic data may also be sent to the cloud for analysis, but this is a separate process from machine data. Both machine and genomic data can be configured for sharing and storage location preferences.

Once in the cloud, Illumina software schedules ETL (extraction, transformation and loading) tasks for the machine data. ETL is the general process of extracting data from source systems and bringing it into a data warehouse. In this case, data is merely being reformatted from flat files and loaded in the Amazon RedShift data warehouse. The collection architecture supports ETL processing using multiple compute instances if necessary. RedShift is optimized for querying columnar data to extract single metrics very efficiently and is useful for querying large amounts of data. An example query might be to see the signal intensity across sequencing runs for a particular instrument, looking for any emerging problems with the light source or optical systems on that instrument.

Genomic data is not being loaded into RedShift but instead is stored in separate tools optimized for researching and analyzing genomic data, such as Illumina's NextBio suite. In addition to being optimized for analyzing these large data sets, these tools also handle requirements like patient privacy and medical-data security.

Learn

The machine data allows Illumina to calculate instrument utilization, uptime and downtime metrics. They are able to discern customer behavior, software adoption, system-fault frequencies and gene-sequencer performance. Currently they are using a variety of visualization software including ThingWorx, Tableau, and JMP from SAS. An example would be analyzing the sequencing quality scores. Sequencing quality scores measure the probability that a base is called incorrectly. A quality score of 20 represents an error rate of 1 in 100, with a corresponding call accuracy of 99%.

The quality score is one of the run-based measurements, which Illumina monitors across the installed base of gene sequencers. Box plots are created using the visualization software. A box plot is a standardized way of displaying the distribution of data based on the five number summaries: minimum, first quartile, median, third quartile, and maximum. The results are charted over time; last year the quality engineers noticed a statistically significant drop in field quality scores. Further investigation led them to realize there was a problem with a batch of reagents. Future analysis targets trends in performance of optics, filters or lasers to identify cases where equipment might be starting to underperform. Machine learning and these analytic engines are part of the project roadmap.

Do

Illumina provides a wide range of service plans listed in Figure 18.3. These services will vary the average response time from five business days to immediate, dedicated, on-site service people, whether parts are included or there are preventive maintenance visits. About 70% of their customers purchase some level of service. Advances in technology should both increase the quality and decrease the cost of delivering these services.

Illumina Product Care Service Plan Comparison

	Parts Only	Basic	Comprehensive	Advantage	Dedicated Onsite	Dx[a]
Terms (Years)	1	1	1	1	2	1
Replacement Parts	Yes	Yes	Yes	Yes	Parts Only Contract Required[a]	Yes
Replacement Reagents for Instrument Failure	No	Yes	Yes	Yes	Yes	Yes
Labor[b]	No	Yes	Yes	Yes	Yes	Yes
5 x 24 Email Support	Yes	Yes	Yes	Yes	Yes	Yes
5 x 18 Email Support[c]	Yes	Yes	Yes	Yes	Yes	Yes
Average Onsite Response Time (Business Days)	5 (from Service PO Receipt)	5	3	2	Immediate	3
Preventive Maintenance	No	No	1	1	2[d]	1
Qualification	No	No	No	Yes[e]	No	Yes
Software/Hardware Updates	No	Yes	Yes	Yes	Yes	Yes
Applications Support[f]	No	Yes	Yes	Yes	Yes	Yes
Advanced Applications Training	No	Discounts Available	Discounts Available	Discounts Available	Discounts Available	Discounts Available

Figure 18.4 Illumina Service Plans

The most significant cost of a hospital or clinic that uses Illumina machines to provide services is the cost of reagents. Illumina's new HiSeq X Ten will be able to get close to a $1,000 per genome. A recent article in Nature Magazine[4] quoted the CEO's breakdown of the cost of a sequence to include $797 for the reagents, $137 for the depreciated cost of the gene sequencer and between $55–65 in technician labor to prepare the samples and manage the machines. In

---

[4] http://www.nature.com/news/is-the-1-000-genome-for-real-1.14530

the airline industry, fuel can account for up to 40% of the operational cost. A variety of technologies are being applied to continue to improve on fuel efficiency. Similarly, advances in technology will be key to arriving at $100 per sequence and opening up even bigger genomic applications.

19

Precision Agriculture

Every time you get on an airplane, one of your first decisions is whether or not to talk to your seatmate. About a year ago I was getting on the long, 12-hour flight from Chennai to Frankfurt, which boards at midnight, and decided it would be more fun to talk than to try to sleep. After the usual pleasantries, I asked my seatmate whom he worked for and he said AGCO. Four hours later, Paul Blackmore, who has worked for AGCO for more than twenty years, taught me more about the tractor and farm-equipment business than I ever knew.

AGCO Corporation is a multi-billion-dollar manufacturer of agricultural equipment. The company makes tractors, including high-horsepower tractors used on larger farms, utility tractors for small and medium-sized farms, and compact tractors for small farms, landscaping and residential uses. The company produces combines used in harvesting grain crops such as corn, wheat, soybean and rice products. It also provides equipment for the application of wet and dry fertilizers and crop protection chemicals, and chemical sprayer equipment used during the planting of crops and after they emerge from the soil. It markets its products under the Challenger, Fendt, GSI, Massey Ferguson and Valtra brands through a network of independent dealers and distributors.

Things

While there are many kinds of farm machines, here we'll focus on a recently released Gleaner-brand combine, which is a transverse rotary harvester. A combine is a machine that harvests grain crops. The name is derived from combining three separate operations — reaping, threshing and winnowing — into a single process. Reaping is the cutting of the grain stalks; threshing is separating the grain from the stalks; and winnowing is separating the grain from the chaff. Among the crops harvested with a combine are wheat, oats, rye, barley, corn, sorghum, soybeans and canola. Combines account for 6% of AGCO's overall revenues.

Figure 19.1 AGCO Gleaner

The combine has a color, touch-screen interface so operators can monitor and control multiple combine functions, many with a single touch. The machine also provides farmers with live-yield mapping, which integrates data from yield and moisture sensors with global positioning information.

One of the elements that can be controlled on the combine is the header width, which is what you see in front of the combine in Figure 19.1. The farmer must set up the header width for the harvester and match it with his yield map to enable yield calculations, which are thrown off when the header is partially loaded with grain. This can happen during a turn or when a field doesn't tie out to a full header width on one or more lines in the field. With variable width control, the combine automatically calculates the yield based on the header load, therefore accurately reporting the yield. The combine is equipped with a number of sensors; for example, Figure 19.2 is a sample set.

Variable Name	Source
Engine Hours	Engine ECU
Vehicle Speed	Transmission sensor
Harvest Hours	PTO ECU
Engine Speed	RPM sensor
Fuel Level	% from fuel tank
Fuel Rate	Engine ECU
DEF Level	% from DEF tank
Engine Coolant Temp	Engine temp sensor
Engine Oil Pressure	Oil pressure sensor
Engine Load	Engine ECU
Chaffer Position	Linear position sensor
Concave Position	Linear position sensor
Sieve Position	Linear position sensor
Grain Loss, Shoe	Calculated
Grain Loss, Rotor	Calculated
Header Height	Linear position sensor
Rotor Speed	RPM sensor
Reel Speed	RPM sensor
Fan Speed	RPM Sensor
Unload Auger Status	On/off sensor
Yield Instant	Load cell
Yield Average	Load cell
Moisture Instant	Conductivity sensor
Moisture Average	Conductivity sensor
Capacity Instant	Calculated
Capacity Average	Calculated
Guidance Status (Automatic steering)	Machine BUS
Test Weight	User input
In Work	Machine ECU calculation

Figure 19.2 Data from the AGCO Combine

As AGCO wants to both connect new and current machines, they have engineered the AGCO Connectivity Module (ACM). ACM contains a dual-core AMD A9 processor with 4GB of RAM running a

Linux platform. It also interfaces to Trimble Navigation, TopCon Positioning Systems and Novatel Inc. for location information.

Connect

The primary connection technology used is 2G and 3G cellular. In standard mode, data is logged and transferred every minute. In advanced mode, data is sampled and transmitted six times per minute. If the combine cannot connect to the server via the cellular network, it will automatically use satellite transfer mode after one minute. Once this happens, the data transfer will occur only once every twelve hours. While in satellite mode, data is accumulated on the combine for transmission. As soon as the combine is driven into an area with cell coverage, it will send all the stored data to the AGCO servers. AGCO uses the Iridium satellite network to achieve global connection services. The connection cost is embedded in the AGCO service and they have developed an option to select a data plan based on intended hours of use instead of just by year.

Collect

AGCO provides what they call a "two-pipe" approach in dealing with data generated through its equipment. The two-pipes are agronomic and machine data. Machine data, if the customer chooses, can be shared with AGCO and at the dealership level. They are currently storing data in raw form in a SQL database running on Microsoft Azure's cloud service.

As for agronomic data, a second pipe is used to transmit sensitive farm information, such as prescription maps, yield maps, applied data and planning data. That information is not stored by AGCO; instead, they have developed a set of APIs to allow it to be pulled by Farm Works' Farm Management Information System.

Learn

Both dealers and operators of the machines use the collected data.

Figure 19.3 Fleet Dashboard

Figure 19.3 shows an overview of all machines in an account. This screen allows the dealer or the farmer to quickly take a glance at which machines within the fleet require attention. Machines can be sorted from highest to lowest in priority based on the amount and severity of un-resolved notifications.

As shown in Figure 19.4, for any particular machine, a notification may be the trigger of a threshold alert such as Engine Coolant Temperature. Alert levels have been pre-populated by AGCO and assigned a level of severity.

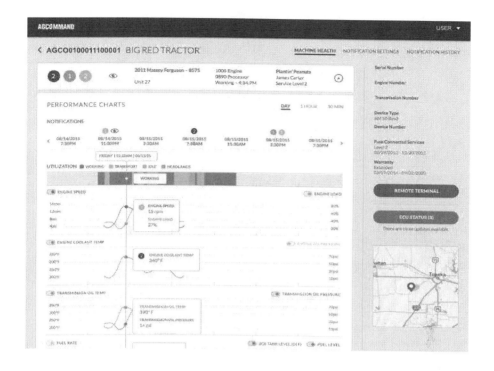

Figure 19.4 Machine Dashboard

If the machine has triggered a threshold alert that indicates a potential machine failure, the dealer can notify the customer to be sure the machine is stopped, potentially avoiding any serious machine issues and thus minimizing the risk of downtime. The dealer can make recommendations of how to run the machine in a way that does not risk it going down, or the dealer can send a service technician to replace parts if needed. Given the machine is geo-located, deploying a dealer technician is much easier.

In addition, using the data can both minimize input costs associated with a machine (fuel, parts, etc.) and maximize output from a particular machine. In the case of minimizing equipment-input costs, fuel use is the first thing a farmer will look to improve. Seeing summary reports on a machine-by-machine basis lets them identify if fuel use is too high. Being able to drill down and look at fuel use against other parameter values — such as speed, RPM and engine load — may facilitate the reduction of fuel consumption. In some cases it may be as simple as identifying that the machine was not run efficiently because there was an inexperienced operator in the cab. Operator training may be a quick fix to save money over the course of a season.

In the case of maximizing output, you could use the measurement of engine load. If an engine is rated for a certain horsepower, engine load is how much of that horsepower the engine is outputting. If you exceed 100%, you could risk an engine stalling. On the other hand, if you're pulling a planter (planters are used to plant single corn or bean seeds) and operating at 50% engine load, you're underutilizing your equipment and thus not getting your money's worth. By reporting on engine load for a particular machine across a season, you may be able to make better implement-pairing decisions. Learning from this information can lead you to either purchase a smaller tractor upon trade in (save money on equipment investment) or a larger planter (save time planting; make the most out of the equipment you have).

Do

AGCO is using the technology to enable its dealer channel to provide higher levels of service. Comper, an agricultural machine dealer in Brazil, supplies its sugar-cane-mill customers with large fleets of multiple machine types year-round and service over 200 machines in the field. By connecting farm machines they are able to improve the quality and reduce the cost of service and have even pioneered new business models.

Improve the Quality of Service to Farmers

Comper delivers on service contracts, which provide for scheduled maintenance and pre-season inspections. By connecting to the machines they are able to monitor them and define standards for machine operation. Furthermore, they are providing assisted services through operation consultation and decision support. All of this results in Comper being able to guarantee a minimum of 87% machine uptime.

Augustin, a dealer with medium-sized customers, is providing assisted services and making recommendations to clients on how to improve uptime using data analytics. They are providing the service for combines and sprayers.

Reduce the Cost of Service

Comper is also able to reduce the cost of service versus the farmers doing it themselves. With nearly sixty service technicians on staff, they are able to specialize and operate at 93% productivity. Any single farmer would do well do keep a technician utilized even 50% of the time, resulting in at least twice the cost — and we're not even talking about the quality of work.

New Business Models

By being able to connect machines and provide assistance in increasing the reliability and performance of the machines, it's only logical that Comper provides agricultural machines as a service. Today they offer tractors-as-a-service for large customers; these tractors are sold by the hour, with a minimum of a few thousand hours per year. Comper takes care of everything other than providing the driver and guarantees an 87% machine uptime.

Finally, AGCO is also going direct to some of its customers with its new sugar-cane-harvester machines, which can cost $250,000 or more. Along with the latest machines, they are connecting them all to a centralized facility to make optimization recommendations to the farmer as well as beginning to implement predictive maintenance. Perhaps in time we'll see a sugar harvester as a service.

20

Precision Buildings

I grew up in the great state of North Carolina so whenever I hear a Southern accent, it brings back many fond memories. As so it was when I got on the phone with Leroy Walden, Vice President of McKenney's Inc. McKenney's is a mechanical contractor in the Southeast that offers a full range of services, including heating, ventilating and air conditioning (HVAC), process piping, plumbing, service and maintenance, and building automation and control systems. As Leroy tells the story, in early 2012, McKenney's joined Gulf Power and Chevron Energy Solutions to implement a new energy management system at Eglin Air Force Base (Eglin). Eglin, at 724 square miles, is one of the largest military bases in the world, and includes hundreds of buildings and a base population of about 17,000.

Things

Eglin has thousands of devices from disparate manufacturers and protocols, including a very large HVAC control system and wireless-power-metering infrastructure. In aggregate, there are 20,000 sensors and data inputs in more than 100 buildings.

SA.BLDG1-5.BTU.MTR:SUPPLYTEMP	013 2 09 05	( )	43.55	1DGF
SA.BLDG1-5.BTU.MTR:RETURNTEMP	013 2 09 06	( )	53.26	1DGF
SA.BLDG6.BTU.MTR:ENERGY RATE	013 3 01 03	( )	1744	KBPH
SA.BLDG1-5.BTU.MTR:VOLUME RATE	013 2 09 04	( )	1763	1GPM
SA.BLDG6.BTU.MTR:SUPPLYTEMP	013 3 01 05	( )	44.07	1DGF
SA.BLDG6.BTU.MTR:RETURNTEMP	013 3 01 06	( )	51.33	1DGF
SA.BLDG1-5.BTU.MTR:ENERGY RATE	013 2 09 03	( )	8289	KBPH
SA.BLDG6.BTU.MTR:VOLUME RATE	013 3 01 04	( )	536	1GPM
SA.CP.CHW.SWT	013 0 00 21	(CHILL WTR SUPPLY)	44.25	deg F
SA.CP.CHW.RWT	013 0 00 20	(CHILL WTR RETURN)	51.05	deg F
SA.CP.CHP03.SPEED	001 0 09 01	(PUMP SPEED)	0	%
SA.CP.CHP04.SPEED	001 0 09 02	(PUMP SPEED)	0	%
SA.CP.CHP06.SPEED	001 0 11 01	(PUMP SPEED)	0	%
SA.CP.CHP08.SPEED	001 0 11 02	(PUMP SPEED)	0	%
SA.CP.CHP09.SPEED	013 0 00 13	(PUMP 9 SPEED)	87.54	%
SA.CP.CHP10.SPEED	013 0 00 14	(PUMP 10 SPEED)	87.54	%
SA.PH1.CP.CH01.SUPTMP	001 0 33 01	(CHILL 1 SUPPLY)	48.01	DEG F
SA.PH1.CP.CH02.SUPTMP	001 0 33 02	(CHILL 2 SUPPLY)	46.58	DEG F

Figure 20.1 McQuay Chiller Data

An example of one kind of machine is the McQuay Chiller. In air conditioning systems, chilled water is typically distributed to heat exchangers (or coils) in air-handling units or other types of terminal devices, which cools the air in the respective space(s); then the water is re-circulated back to the chiller to be cooled again. The chiller sensors continuously report on chilled-water-supply temperature, chilled-water-return temperature and flow status, logging in 15-minute intervals. An example of the kind of data is shown in Figure 20.1.

A variety of other sensors are also on the base, including the Sensus FlexNet electric meters, which continuously read power metrics (e.g., kVA and kVAh). The meters are deployed on outlying buildings that have no building automation. In addition, Schneider Electric's room thermostat continuously provides space temperature and humidity and occupancy status, logged in 15-minute intervals.

The Johnson Controls' Variable Air Volume (VAV) controller continuously provides airflow, discharge-air temperature, damper position and heat-output readings, which are logged in 15-minute intervals. VAV is a type of HVAC system that, unlike constant air volume (CAV) systems — which supply a constant airflow at a variable temperature — vary the airflow at a constant temperature. The advantages of VAV systems over CAV systems include more precise temperature control, reduced compressor wear, lower energy consumption by system fans, reduced fan noise and additional passive dehumidification.

Connect

Eglin uses Tridium Niagara Framework to connect many of these machines. Tridium provides a multi-vendor interoperable control system that satisfies the need for Internet openness while maintaining the determinism and integrity required for real-time control. To be deterministic means that every time the same function occurs, it must happen in exactly the same way and at exactly the same speed.

For example, consider a building outfitted with a smart electrical meter that provides the current, real-time price of electricity being used and a chiller that controls the temperature. Independently, the electrical meter and the chiller cannot communicate; however, when joined together using a standard communications and applications infrastructure — such as the Niagara Framework — it becomes possible to vary the building temperature and thus vary chiller energy consumption in accordance with energy prices.

The key elements of the framework include database management, security, web server, browser-user interface, real-time control engine, enterprise support and a complete application-development environment. There is also a hardware component. The Java Application Control Engine (JACE) controllers are a series of embedded computer hardware devices that act in an area-controller capacity to distribute real-time-control functions across an Ethernet bus in a large system.

JACE connects three of the most widely used connection protocols today: BACnet, LonMark and Modbus. While all three have been used successfully in implementing interoperable building automation systems, the approaches to interoperability are vastly different.

For connection security, the U.S. government has mandated that bases remove their building controls infrastructure to a 'dark fiber' segmented network. Network hardware is monitored by an InterMapper server that resides on the segmented network. The InterMapper server monitors network data such as device downtime and available bandwidth. Electric-power-meter data from the Sensus devices operate on a 900MHz radio spectrum. McKenney's created a custom Niagara application that collects the data from specified points and writes to a .log file that is monitored by Splunk.

Collect

Sensus meter data is collected in a SQL server then passed to the Splunk indexer. HVAC data is collected in 15-minute increments and power-meter data is collected continuously in real-time by Sensus. The indexer also collects information from flat files that can be manually input, as well as log files from the Niagara AX system and InterMapper server.

Splunk performs real-time and historical search, reports and statistical analysis. The product can index structured or unstructured, textual, machine-generated data. Search and analytics operations are specified using their Search Processing Language. Originally based upon Unix Piping and SQL, its scope includes data searching, filtering, modification, manipulation, insertion and deletion. Eglin data is being archived via Splunk Enterprise with a three-year data-retention policy.

Splunk runs on a dedicated server on Eglin's private network and all site data feeds into and is collected by a Splunk indexer. A Splunk search head resides on another server and allows users to access and create custom searches and reports.

Learn

By correlating both historical and real time energy utilization and pricing data with occupancy and environmental data from the HVAC, the base identified significant opportunities for load shedding, such as times it can shut off select HVAC systems during high energy cost periods.

Splunk is also being used to analyze the data. Data is analyzed continuously and on-demand as requested by the users. Initial functionality focused on utility visualization and cost allocation. Insights are being gained relative to structure-performance baselines. For example, what is the efficiency of a wood frame versus concrete block buildings? Subsequent phases will incorporate predictive analytics and automated, cost-management routines.

Do

Leroy's team built an energy management application that provides dashboards to help Eglin's maintenance staff assess building performance and energy efficiency, generate automated Air Force and DoD energy usage reports, compare current energy usage with historical data, and enable the deployment of load shedding and load shifting strategies to take advantage of favorable electric rates. All of this leads to more precise building management, lower costs and improved service, health and safety.

Lower Consumables Cost

The U.S. Department of Energy's Federal Energy Management Program (FEMP) chose Eglin as the recipient of a 2015 energy and water conservation award. The award recognizes Eglin's innovative approach for combining advanced technologies and common sense to saving critical energy resources and reducing utility costs for the base. By integrating direct digital controls, facility meters, and comprehensive energy analyses, the project saved 181-billion BTUs of electricity and natural gas across 131 buildings, valued at $3.4M.

Higher Quality Service

The technology also has the ability to improve the quality of service. For example, if boilers, chillers, variable air-volume systems or other building maintenance components are not performing optimally, the building service department can proactively fix these hardware issues, avoiding even more expensive service calls.

Improved Health and Safety

From a safety perspective, one aspect is that many of the meters being read and recorded are located in mid-field equipment buildings, which require personnel on active runways to diagnose problems and read data. Clearly, this is no longer necessary.

21

Precision Construction

The first time I heard the term "19-foot scissor" was in a meeting with a construction equipment rental company, I thought they must mean a 19-*inch* scissor. Of course, that led to the question, "Why would anyone want to rent a 19-inch scissor?" As is with any industry, you have to learn the language, so after the laughter died down, I learned it was a 19-foot scissor lift, which you've likely seen being used to replace light bulbs in high ceilings.

This construction equipment rental company offers thousands of classes of equipment to construction and industrial companies, manufacturers, utilities, municipalities, and even homeowners. Construction machines include backhoes, skid-steer loaders, forklifts, and earthmoving equipment; aerial-work platforms consisting of boom lifts and scissor lifts; and general tools and lighting equipment, including pressure washers, water pumps and power tools. The equipment can be highly specialized and used for many purposes. Consider the case of a hydronic surface heater (aka: a ground heater), which was designed to warm soil during a concrete pour in the winter. While that was its main purpose, an enterprising group also realized it could be used to heat community pools, adding another month of usage on both ends of the summer season.

More and more, construction equipment rental companies are becoming digital to increase the level of service and decrease the delivery costs for their clients. With assets valued at over $10B, small changes can make a big difference.

Things

- Amps Phase A (ST_AMPS_A)
- Amps Phase B (ST_AMPS_B)
- Amps Phase C (ST_AMPS_C)
- Apparent Power (ST_KVA)
- Cellular Signal % (CELL_SIGNAL)

Engel Inverter Diesel Generator

- Percent Amps B (ST_PCT_AMPS_B)
- Percent Amps C (ST_PCT_AMPS_C)
- Power Factor (ST_POWER_FA)
- Power in KVAR (ST_KVAR)
- Total KW (ST_KW)

- Check Genset (AL_CHK)
- Common Alarm (AL_COMN)
- Control Panel - Ignition Switch (ST_IGNIT_SW)
- Control Switch (ST_CONTROL)
- Device Type (ST_DEVICE)
- Emergency Stop (AL_ESTOP)
- Engine Coolant Temperature - Coolant Temperature (ST_COTE)
- Engine Oil Pressure - Oil Pressure (ST_OIL_PR)
- Engine On Time - Run Hours (ST_RUN_HS)
- Engine RPM - Engine RPM (Actual) (ST_RPM)
- Engine Shutdown Alarm (AL_SD_RUN)
- Engine Starts (ST_START_CNT)
- Engine Status (S
- Frequency (ST_FREQ)
- Fuel Level (FUEL_LEVEL)
- Genset Supplying Load (ST_LOAD_GS)
- Last Communication (COMM_TIME)
- Last Data Collection Time (LAST_DATA)
- Low Coolant Temperature (AL_COTE_LOLO)
- Modbus Communication Failure (AL_MODBUS_FL)
- Percent Amps A (ST_PCT_AMPS_A)
- Total Percent kW (ST_KW_PCT)Voltage Phase A-B (ST_VOLT_A)
- Voltage Phase B-C (ST_VOLT_B)
- Voltage Phase C-A (ST_VOLT_C)
- Volts AB - Input Voltage Phase A (ST_VOLTS_A_IN)
- Volts BC - Input Voltage Phase B (ST_VOLTS_B_IN)
- Volts CA - Input Voltage Phase C (ST_VOLTS_C_IN

Figure 21.1 Generator Data

In the world of heavy equipment, SAE J1939 is the business standard, used for communication and diagnostics among vehicle components. Originating in the car and heavy-duty truck industry in the U.S., it is now widely used in other parts of the world and is similar to the ODB2 interface used for automobile data.

While many original equipment manufacturers (OEMs) are starting to provide their own sensors and local computing, some construction rental companies are standardizing on their own designs, rather than deal with the heterogeneous nature of using an OEM's solution. If you have 3,000 different types of machines, this makes a lot of sense.

Companies such as Calamp provide products such as the LMU-5000 as a core component for standardizing across many different types of Things. The LMU-5000 uses a 32-bit 400Mhz ARM processor with 128MB of flash storage. Furthermore, it runs a Linux operating system and provides higher-level services like TCP/IP, HTTP and VPN. And all of this has to be packaged for a construction environment with temperature, humidity, shock and vibration challenges. Each machine can deliver a wide variety of data. Figure 21.1, shows all of the data coming from sensors in a particular generator.

Connect

Products like the LMU-5000 also provide lower-level connectivity, in particular, 3G Tri-Band, packet radio, WiFi and Iridium, and multi-band High Speed Packet Access (HSPA). HSPA is a 3rd-generation (3G) technology offering faster data-download speeds. Updates from the machines can occur from once per hour to once per minute.

Collect

Data is collected from the machines in a connection service provider's SQL database. Today, it's purged on a regular basis. To get a sense of scale, a rental company that has 425,000 machines in the field and data collected once per hour has the equivalent of one NASDAQ's worth of data. Why one NASDAQ? On a typical trading day the NASDAQ processes around ten million transactions. Each transaction is a buy or sell, with a stock ticker symbol and a price. So 425,000 machines reporting data once per hour for 24 hours is 10,200,000 transactions, and as we've seen, some of this data may be much larger.

Once-per-hour data may be pulled into an enterprise resource planning (ERP) application. ERP applications can be very specific to managing rental businesses. For example, consider Wynne Systems' RentalMan; as an ERP application, RentalMan supports the standard accounting processes of accounts payable, accounts receivable and general ledger. You can also manage depreciation of individual or bulk items, billing, taxes and more in multiple countries and currencies. Inventory tracking monitors and logs new equipment and parts purchases, the location of the equipment at any given time, rented equipment and what is coming back to the yard. Finally, the ERP application can also track assets utilization and determine profitability so a construction equipment rental company knows when to buy, move or sell the equipment.

In many cases, data is also pulled into a data warehouse from the ERP system once per day for reporting and analytics. Some companies may use Teradata for their data warehouse; Teradata historically built special purpose hardware and software designed for querying large amounts of data. They utilize a shared-nothing architecture, which means that each server node has its own memory and processing power. Adding more servers and nodes increases the amount of data that can be stored. Their special-purpose, database software spreads the workload among the server nodes and, in the optimal scenario, scales linearly. eBay, a long-time Teradata customer, has thousands of people using its data warehouse, turning over 1Tb every eight seconds as part of its efforts to more efficiently match sellers with buyers.

Learn

The Teradata database is used to learn what kinds (category and brand) of units to purchase, how many to purchase and where to locate them.

When purchasing the equipment, they often have many choices between brands. Each brand has a different purchase cost, annual maintenance cost and resale value. By using historical data collected in the data warehouse, it can estimate which brand is more cost efficient over the life of the equipment, which can have a significant impact on the bottom line.

Within each branch, demand for any equipment can vary over time. Safety stock (also called buffer stock) is a term used by logisticians to describe a level of extra stock that is maintained to mitigate risk of not having the equipment available. Of course, ensuring that 100% of customers will be able to rent a particular piece of equipment would drive inventory artificially high. Using the data collected, and based on past demand and appropriate service level, the company can estimate the necessary safety stock.

Finally, because it's costly to move large construction equipment around, the company uses the data to help determine the optimal location. Equipment can be managed at the local or regional level; when equipment is managed at a higher level, it gives more flexibility and less variability but higher transportation cost. Understanding variability and transportation-cost tradeoff by equipment can help decide where the equipment should be managed.

Do

Connecting the construction equipment is valuable to the machine-providing company in that it reduces the cost and improves the quality of service.

Reduce the Cost of Service
One simple example is being able to know where the equipment is located. In the unconnected state, the machines don't know where they are and can't tell the rental company, which results in wasted time and money when trying to pick up the machines.

Being able to monitor the equipment and learn when maintenance should occur — rather than following a strict, time-based maintenance stream — can dramatically improve financial performance. In most rental companies, the ongoing maintenance of the machines is the single largest operating cost. We intuitively know a machine operated incorrectly in adverse conditions will need significantly more frequent maintenance than one that is operated infrequently in a benign environment. Being able to precisely identify the ones needing more frequent or less frequent maintenance could easily save $100M annually on a $1B spend.

Improve the Quality of Service
Most construction rental companies charge when equipment is used beyond eight hours per day. Without any connection to the equipment and the customer, the current practice is a very large bill at the end of the rental, which is often written off. In the connected state, the company can notify the customer via a portal and other

communications when the equipment is used more than eight hours per day.

Beyond that, if you could improve the availability, performance and security of the machines by providing assistance and advice or directly managing them, the value to the customer of the machine also rises. This is only possible in the connected state where you are collecting and learning from the data of thousands of machines.

The use of precision construction machines on a construction project can also result in more precise construction by lowering consumables cost and improving the end product and the health and safety of the construction crew.

Lower Consumables Cost

The ability to collect data about the machines can lead to lower energy costs of operating them. Collected information can also lead to ensuring that you have the optimal number of machines at a site, thereby reducing the need to rent the equipment at all. It might seem counter intuitive, but if you think better service leads to higher customer retention, then factoring in the cost of sales is going to result in more business.

Higher Quality Product or Service

Offering a customer visibility into the state of their construction machines can provide significant value. This includes visibility to equipment utilization along with text alerts when equipment is past due, notifications on low equipment utilization and the ability to define and record off-rent dates. In some situations, customers who fully utilize the information may save up to one third on annual rental costs, which results in either higher margin to the construction company or a higher quality building at a lower cost.

Furthermore, connected machines can enable their supplier to make recommendations on what kinds of equipment might best suit this phase of the construction project and make them available in a timely manner, further improving the quality and reducing the cost of the overall project.

Improved Health and Safety

Connecting construction equipment can also improve safety on the job site, from ensuring that the equipment is functioning properly to being able to predict problems.

22

Precision Healthcare

U.S. News and World Report named UC Irvine Medical one of the nation's top 50 hospitals for gynecology, cancer, digestive disorders and urology. The medical center has been home to a number of firsts — including Orange County's first heart transplant, the West Coast's first insulin pump implant in a patient with diabetes, and a number of research breakthroughs involving therapy for cancer and other diseases.

Under the leadership of Charles Boicey, an informatics solution architect, the medical center has piloted a new technology to frequently monitor and transmit patient vital signs. Patients in the pilot program wore a SensiumVitals patch that monitored and wirelessly transmitted heart rate, respiratory rate and temperature every minute; the objective was to have software that alerted nurses if a patient's vital signs crossed certain risk thresholds so the patient could be immediately attended to.

Things

SensiumVitals is a wireless system designed to monitor the vital signs of patients in all areas of the hospital setting where patients would not normally be continuously monitored. The product is a light-weight, wearable, wireless, single-use patch that takes vital signs and wirelessly communicates that data to clinicians via the hospital's IT infrastructure.

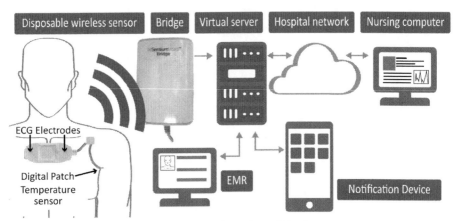

Figure 22.1 SensiumVitals

The system takes patient measurements every two minutes, which is significantly more often than current manual practices where the majority of patients have vital signs taken only once every 4–8 hours. Infrequent monitoring can mean that deterioration in patient conditions may go unnoticed, potentially leading to longer hospital stays, more expensive treatments or even admittance to intensive care.

This patch provides continuous monitoring of three of the patient's vital signs — heart rate, respiration rate and temperature — with a high degree of accuracy. The patches transmit data every two minutes, which is about 4,320 data points per patient, per day.

The patch's processing power is a proprietary Sensium system-on-a-chip (SoC), which is based on the 8051 microcontroller — a complex instruction set computing (CISC) instruction set, single-chip-microcontroller series developed by Intel in 1980 for use in embedded systems. The Sensium implementation runs at 16MHz with a 32kHz sleep clock. The patch is disposable and has no operating system; they don't need to do software updates often, although they can update the software through the electrode snaps post-production if required. Normally, they just make changes to the next batch of patches when they're produced.

Connect

The patch is connected to the network through a proprietary ZigBee-like protocol. The ZigBee protocol is a IEEE 802.15.4-based specification for a suite of high-level communication protocols used to create personal area networks with small, low-power digital radios. The technology is intended to be simpler and less expensive than Bluetooth or WiFi. Its low-power consumption does limit transmission distances to 10–100 meters. In the hospital environment they use the hospital ISM band of 915MHz.

The devices can transmit data over long distances by passing it through a mesh network of intermediate devices to reach more distant ones. ZigBee is typically used in low-data-rate applications that require long battery life and secure networking; 128-bit symmetric encryption keys secure ZigBee networks. ZigBee has a defined rate of 250Kbit per second and is best suited for intermittent data transmissions from a sensor or input device. One of the other advantages is that you can get both 2-D position (latitude, longitude) and elevation information so you'll know what floor the device is on. And as a separate radio frequency, there is no interference with WiFi.

As a result of the choice to use ZigBee, Sensium has created a disposable sensor that can be used for five days for a cost of around $50. This saves nurses time, as they don't have to clean equipment or risk contamination between patients as they would have to with a multi-use device. Its low-power consumption allows for reasonably long battery life, meaning nurses don't have to charge or replace batteries. This is compared to some WiFi solutions that cost 50 times more and require that the product is cleaned and charged before it's used with another patient.

Sensium has implemented a bridge to connect the patches to the hospital servers. Unlike Bluetooth, this enables the patch wearer to move around and automatically maintain the connection. The device can also be outside of network coverage for up to three hours and will store vital-sign data on the patch; the data will then upload automatically as soon as the patient comes back into contact with a base station. As a rule of thumb, a typical ward in a hospital requires 10 bridges.

Collect

All of the data is collected in a Hortonworks Hadoop environment running within a VMware instance on an on-premises Dell server. Hadoop is an open-source software framework for distributed storage and distributed processing of very large data sets on computer clusters built from commodity hardware. Hadoop is designed with a fundamental assumption that hardware failures are commonplace and thus should be automatically handled in software by the framework.

The core of Hadoop consists of a storage part (Hadoop Distributed File System, also known as HDFS) and a processing part

(MapReduce). Hadoop splits files into large blocks and distributes them amongst the nodes in the cluster. To process the data, MapReduce transfers packaged code for nodes to process in parallel based on the data each node needs to process. This approach takes advantage of data locality — nodes manipulating the data that they have on hand — to allow the data to be processed faster and more efficiently than it would be in a more conventional architecture. Hadoop was used because it was a simple solution that allowed data to be processed in its native form. Some people think of Hadoop as only being used for large amounts of data, but in this case, 350 patients with a reading every minute creates less than 100Gbytes of data in three years.

At UC Irvine, the data is also collected in an electronic medical record (EMR) application provided by Sunrise, a division of AllScripts. An EMR or electronic health record (EHR) refers to an application that collects and stores patient health information in a digital format. The EMR application may include a range of data, including demographics, medical history, medication and allergies, immunization status, laboratory test results, radiology images, vital signs, personal statistics like age and weight, and billing information.

UC Irvine used NatHealth's DeviceConX to integrate all the devices into the EMR. In many hospitals, data captured by devices is manually entered into the electronic record by clinicians. This manually entered data is often hours old by the time it is keyed in, and transcription errors are inevitable. DeviceConX is a software solution that collects and transmits device data captured from thousands of medical devices, delivering that data to an EMR, CIS or other data repository. In this case, data from the devices is stored in the EMR once every 4–8 hours and previous history is purged every 3–5 days.

Learn

By using three years of historic sensor data coupled with Code Blue and rapid response events, the UC Irvine team built a predictive model. Code Blue is used to indicate a patient requiring resuscitation or in need of immediate medical attention, most often as the result of respiratory or cardiac arrest. The model also uses other sources of data including EMR and lab data.

Three examples of the 16 types of time-series data include SpO2, which measures the amount of oxygen in the blood; more specifically, it is the percentage of oxygenated hemoglobin compared to the total amount of hemoglobin in the blood; pCO2, which measures the partial pressure of carbon dioxide in arterial blood, is a good indicator of respiratory function and reflects the amount of acid in the blood; and NBP systolic, which is measured in milligrams of mercury (mmHG) and is a non-invasive, blood pressure measurement.

A team from Tata Consulting Services built the first models using both ARIMA models and support vector machines written in R: Auto-regressive integrated moving average (ARIMA) models. These are applied in cases where data shows evidence of non-stationarity, where an initial differencing step (corresponding to the "integrated" part of the model) can be applied to reduce the non-stationarity. Support vector machines are supervised learning models with associated learning algorithms that analyze data and recognize patterns and are used for classification and regression analysis. A support vector-machine model is a representation of the examples as points in space, mapped so the examples of the separate categories are divided by a clear gap that is as wide as possible. New examples are then mapped into that same space and predicted to belong to a category based on which side of the gap they fall on.

Do

An ability to precisely monitor patients can have significant health benefits. The Hospital for Sick Children, a leading children's hospital in Toronto, conducted a study of premature, low-birth-weight babies. The study showed about 20% of the children will develop an infection and of those babies, about 18% will die. Physicians theorized that by detecting signals indicating the onset of infection, also called sepsis, they could intervene earlier.

An analysis of data also surprisingly revealed that premature babies with more stable heartbeats were actually more susceptible to infections. Starting 12–24 hours before the onset of noticeable symptoms, the heart rates of infected babies became too regular and stopped varying, as they should in a healthy state.

The results of UC Irvine's work were an ability to predict a Code Blue with reasonable accuracy within 90 seconds of the event. While that's a good first step, the goal is to be able to make a prediction ten minutes into the future. Charles Boicey has gone on to ClearSense to continue this work.

23

Precision Oil and Gas

The oil and gas industry is divided into three major sectors: upstream, midstream and downstream. The upstream oil sector is focused on exploration and production of crude oil and/or natural gas. Recently, unconventional natural gas has been added to the upstream sector, as well as liquefied natural gas (LNG) processing and transport. The midstream involves the transportation (by pipeline, rail, barge, oil tanker or truck), storage and wholesale marketing of crude or natural gas. The downstream sector refers to the refining of petroleum crude oil and the marketing and distribution of products derived from crude oil and natural gas. The downstream sector touches consumers through products such as gasoline, jet fuel, diesel oil, propane fuel and liquefied petroleum gas, in addition to hundreds of petrochemicals.

Upstream is very much a single-product commodity business; even downstream and midstream only have a few ways to differentiate the products. For the purpose of this case, we're going to focus on upstream where there are three asset classes: unconventional (aka: fracking), deep water (aka: offshore oil and gas) and LNG terminals. Historically, deep-water oil and gas platforms are the most instrumented.

Things

Oil and gas production platforms can be huge. Chevron recently deployed a 160,000-ton platform that floats in 7,000 feet of water located 280 miles south of New Orleans. Its wells pierce the Jack and St. Malo reservoirs 26,500 feet below sea level. The platform acts as a hub for 43 subsea wells, which are divided into three clusters comprising subsea wells, pumps and other equipment on the seafloor. For a sense of scale, this kind of platform can take 2,500 welders two years to complete.

There are a variety of Things aboard any platform like pumps, compressors and separators, from a variety of suppliers including General Electric, Siemens, Caterpillar and others. Each of these machines is well instrumented; a modern production platform can have anywhere from 20–40 thousand sensors in place.

Figure 23.1 Rotor from a 3-stage Centrifugal Compressor

One example of equipment on an oil platform is a 3-stage centrifugal compressor. Figure 23.1 shows a maintenance crew placing the rotor back in the casing after some overhaul. The casing is usually split into two halves. In the foreground, you can see the bolts, which are used for aligning the two halves of the casing together. Sensor data from these compressors include:

- Suction and discharge pressures measured in bar gauge — bar(g) — or pounds per square inch gauge (PSIG)
- Suction and discharge temperatures measured in Celsius or Fahrenheit
- Flow measured in cubic meter per hour (MM SCFH)
- Anti-surge or recycle valve positions and controller demands in percentages
- Suction drum levels in inches or percentages
- Lubricating oil pressure measured in bar(g) or PSIG

- Lubricating oil temperature measured in Celsius or Fahrenheit
- Bearing vibrations measured in Microns or Mils

These sensors generate time-series data, alarm and events data, and unstructured data in the form of maintenance and inspection logs.

Connect

Because oil and gas platforms are within line of sight of land, most of the traditional communication has been via microwave. Modern, bigger platforms are all connected by fiber optic cable. On the platform itself, individual sensors are connected using Programmable Logic Controllers (PLCs), which in turn are connected to a network for supervisory control and data acquisition (aka: SCADA network). SCADA networks integrate data acquisition, data transmission and Human-Machine Interface (HMI) software to provide a centralized monitoring and control system for various process inputs and outputs.

Because multiple equipment manufacturers (OEMs) typically provide individual equipment, a common communication standard called OPC (OLE for Process Control) has been developed and is used as a means of communication for connecting individual user interfaces and equipment control systems. These process control networks are also designed as flat networks to facilitate communication between devices with no isolation. Moreover, most industrial control systems are designed for reliability and process safety as opposed to IT networks that are designed for data security. Designed for real-time control, industrial control systems inherently do not focus on running anti-virus software and have multiple pathways through which cyber security threats can enter the network.

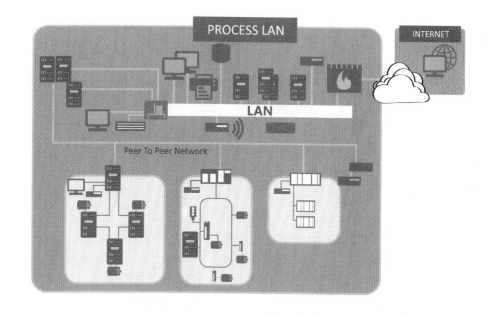

Figure 23.2 Oil-Platform Network

To protect the operations and process control, almost all industrial control systems — including the ones on platforms — implement an architecture that isolates layers of the business and process-control network. The automation and business networks are isolated using managed switches and logical network segregation, which Demilitarized Zones (DMZ) may use to protect the process control system from the Internet and the business network. An example SCADA network topology is shown in Figure 23.2.

Collect

Today, data is collected in many places — almost all SCADA networks have some level of buffering capability where all process data is collected as time-series data. In addition to the SCADA buffers, most platforms have a special database called historian software, which is specifically designed to efficiently store, archive and make available time-series data for trending, charting and reporting purposes. The software has built-in exception and compression algorithms to store high-speed, real-time data without losing the waveform characteristic of the process data. A data point for each input sensor (also called a *tag*) is stored as a time-value pair. In addition to this, historians store metadata information about the sensor such as sensor description, unit of measure and scaling factor. Most historian software also has the ability to create and store derived sensors by performing mathematical operations on raw-field sensors (e.g., calculate the differential pressure or pressure ratio of a compressor stage using suction and discharge pressure sensor measurements). These derived sensors are then used as additional inputs for monitoring, control or accounting purposes.

Some examples of historian software products are PI from OSISoft, Proficy Historian from GE, IP21 from AspenTech, and eDNA and Wonderware from Schneider. All of these historians support communication using the OPC standard in addition to using proprietary communication with an API.

Learn

Over the last five to ten years, a number of technologies and solutions have been developed to make use of the process data being collected with historians. These solutions provide early warning by predicting equipment failures. For example, GE's SmartSignal technology is being used by enterprises in power generation, oil and gas, aviation and mining to monitor almost 30,000 unique machines. At the heart of SmartSignal is a machine-learning algorithm designed for condition-based monitoring of industrial processes.

With SmartSignal, each machine is modeled uniquely by constructing an individualized model from the equipment's own historical data. A model or blueprint is a combination of the sensor data grouped by components and sub-systems as well as a set of apparent failure indications and their signature logic. The theory is each machine in the field behaves uniquely due to subtle differences in operating characteristics and component parts with different life history. These subtle differences are represented in the operating data of the machine. The models put into context the relationships among all relevant parameters, such as load, temperatures, pressures, flows, vibration readings and ambient conditions, which are difficult to characterize using traditional, first-principles-physics based models. During the learning phase, a model is established from normal behavior.

Once a model is created and during the monitoring phase, a time-aligned snapshot of data is extracted every few minutes and compared to the model. The model generates a prediction for each of the modeled sensors. The difference between the current value and the model prediction is then analyzed for statistically abnormal behavior and persistence. The abnormal behavior of one or more sensors is combined to match known fault patterns. Thus, an exception driven advisory is generated whenever the abnormal behavior results in a failure-pattern match. The software is able to dynamically change the priority of any advisory based on the rate of change or corroborating evidence.

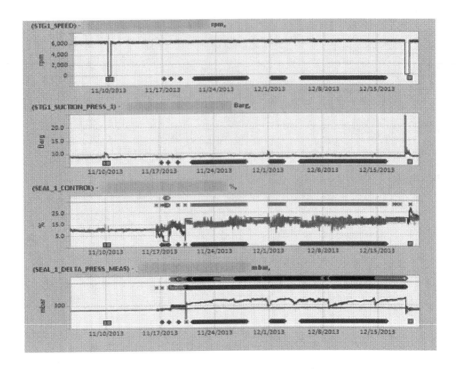

Figure 23.3 SmartSignal Output

Figure 23.3 shows the values of four sensors from a compressor. The blue lines represent the actual value of the sensor being read and the green lines represent the predicted values. From top to bottom, the chart shows Compressor Speed, Suction Pressure, Seal 1 Control Valve Position and Seal 1 Differential Pressure (Pressure between Seal Supply and Compressor Suction). The yellow and red diamonds indicate statistically significant deviations from predicted value. The Seal 1 Differential Control Pressure is the key control parameter to maintain the Seal Pressure as higher than the natural gas pressure inside the case.

Do

The North Sea is one of Europe's largest sources of oil and gas but it can also be a dangerous place; even with oil and gas platforms built sixty feet above sea level, accidents can happen. While the elements are a threat, equipment failure is not only a safety issue, but it can also cause losses in productivity. In November 2013, SmartSignal identified an increase in the seal gas inlet pressure on a 1200HP centrifugal compressor on a North Sea oilrig. Given the loading conditions, the inlet-seal-gas pressure was expected to remain below 300Mbar, but actual values were seen to be higher than the model prediction. Upon notification by GE's Monitoring Center, based outside of Chicago, the operators started tracking the issue closely and scheduled an inspection by a technician at an opportune time. The issue was diagnosed to a malfunctioning seal-gas-control valve. This valve controls and maintains an appropriate seal-gas-inlet pressure to match the compressor flow and discharge pressure.

This early notification allowed the operator to make the decision to place the seal-gas-control system in a manual control and schedule repairs without downtime by isolating the control valve. If left uncorrected, it could have led to a seal failure, potentially resulting in mechanical damage, production losses and negative environmental impacts; in extreme cases, it can even lead to safety issues. Remember, this compressor is just one of hundreds of machines on an oil and gas platform.

In 2015, McKinsey & Company wanted to know how much of the data gathered by sensors on offshore oilrigs is used in decision-making by the energy industry. After studying sensors on rigs around the world, they found that less than one percent of the information gathered from about 30,000 separate data points was being made available to the people in the industry who make decisions. Sebastian Gass at Chevron said most of the data on an oil platform today is "digital exhaust," meaning there is plenty of opportunity to improve the precision of the oil and gas industry.

24

Precision Power

Duke Energy is responsible for providing reliable and affordable electricity to approximately 7.1 million customers across 104,000 square miles and six states. Parts of Florida, Indiana, North Carolina, Kentucky, Ohio and South Carolina are under the Duke Energy umbrella. In order to cover this load, they own approximately 50GW of generation capacity provided mostly by hydro, nuclear, coal-fired, combustion-turbine and combined-cycle power.

This case discusses the use of a particular kind of Thing — a phasor measurement unit (PMU) — which is a device that measures the electrical waves on an electricity grid using a common time source for synchronization. Time synchronization allows synchronized, real-time measurements of multiple remote measurement points on the grid. The resulting measurement is known as a *synchrophasor*. Some think PMUs can revolutionize the way power systems are managed and controlled. A PMU can be a dedicated device, or the function can be incorporated into a protective relay or other device. Duke Energy's vision is to integrate the PMUs into system protection, system planning and system operations to provide more reliable power. The plan in the Carolinas is to install up to 104 PMUs at 52 substations, providing 100% coverage of 500kV buses, 230kV buses and 500kV lines, as well as 60% of 230kV lines.

Things

PMU technology was introduced more than 30 years ago but did not get much attention until the Northeast blackout of 2003, where it became clear that more detailed monitoring capability for the electricity grid was needed. The American Recovery and Reinvestment Act (ARRA) of 2009 (think back to the Great Recession of 2008) paved the way for wide deployment of the technology in the U.S. transmission grid.

PMUs take measurements at the power, frequency, voltage, current and phasor angle (i.e. where you are on the power sine wave). Previous systems only took readings every 3–4 seconds. On the other hand, modern devices now take readings at a speed of 60 times per second, resulting in over 200 times the amount of data. This more frequent interval provides a much more detailed view of the power grid and allows detection of sub-second changes that were completely missed before.

Because these measurements are time-series information and it's important to know that the power is identical at every point in the grid, accurate time measurements are vital. PMUs have GPS receivers built in, not to determine the location, but so all can get the same, accurate time signal. This is sufficient because GPS systems provide time accuracy in the nano-second range, and this accuracy is most critical in the measurement of phasor angles. By comparing the phasor angles between locations, you can get a measure of the power flow between the locations.

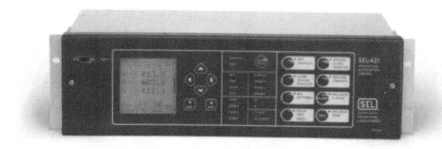

Figure 24.1 Phase Measurement Unit

An example of a PMU is the SEL-421, produced by Schweitzer Engineering Labs. The SEL-421 uses multiple processing devices in a parallel architecture, including an embedded microprocessor, a digital signal processing microprocessor and an FPGA. Its operating system is designed for real-time applications. Software is also packaged to run Ethernet communications and web severs.

Connect

Typically, data from each PMU is reported to a Phasor Data Collector (PDC) via TCP/IP and stored for analysis.

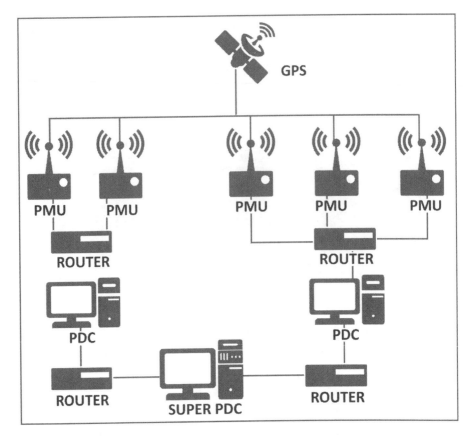

Figure 24.2 PMU Network

Figure 24.2 shows the structure of a typical PMU network. Once PMUs synchronize with the GPS, each measurement sent across the network includes a time stamp. Electrical-distribution line measurements are sent by PMUs over a network connection to a PDC. The PMU communications standard is the IEEE 5C37.118 protocol, which defines data conventions, measurement accuracies and communication formats.

PMUs and PDCs need to be shielded from the larger network; a security gateway is typically implemented to provide an interface between the critical network components and the Internet. These gateways (firewalls) should have three main properties: all traffic must enter; only trusted traffic may pass; and the firewall is immune to penetration. This includes traffic from the PMU to the PDC and vice versa. If a component tries to connect to the PMU or PDC that is not on the trusted list, then it is not allowed to pass. The other job of the security gateway is to establish a VPN connection between substations, which allows measurement and configuration data to be sent securely between substations. Typically, the data is encrypted as it's sent across the network and when it reaches the designated security gateway, the gateway checks to see if the packets were delayed or replayed and decipher the packet. The measurements are then recorded in the PDC's database. PMUs and PDCs are subject to common vulnerabilities, including denial of service, physical, man-in-the-middle, packet analysis, malicious code injection and data-spoofing attacks.

Former ABC News anchor, Ted Koppel, wrote a book called *Lights Out: A Cyberattack, A Nation Unprepared, Surviving the Aftermath*. In a recent interview he said, "Back in 2010, ten former senior top officials — two former directors of the CIA, two former secretaries of defense, two former national security advisers — wrote a letter to a congressional committee. It was a secret letter, which spelled out their findings after dealing with the best experts they could find within the government. They came to the conclusion that tens of millions of people, in the wake of a cyberattack on one of the grids, could be without power for a period up to two years."

Collect

Time-series data from Duke's many machines are collected in an OSISoft PI time-series database; however, in this particular case, where data is solely coming from the PMUs, it is first being stored in a proprietary SAS file structure; SAS Enterprise Miner uses this database for learning and analysis. Once the learning is complete, the execution is managed through SAS's Event Stream Processing (ESP). By definition, ESP software does not collect data and only processes it as it arrives. ESP technologies include event visualization, event databases, event-driven middleware and event-processing languages. ESP products enable many different applications such as algorithmic trading in financial services, RFID event-processing applications, fraud detection, process monitoring, and location-based services in telecommunications.

Learn

The amount of data measured and sent to the PDC at 60 samples per second from each PMU is far too much for the operator to make any sense of on a real-time basis. SAS Enterprise Miner was used to build a decision tree surrounding the PMU measurements. The main purpose is to detect and understand events that are affecting the power grid, with the objective of keeping the grid stable. They have learned there are a number of time-series techniques that are necessary for the different aspects of providing the needed answers. The analysis flow breaks down into three areas: Did something happen? What happened? How bad was it?

Event Detection
For event detection, the PMUs generate 60 measurements per second on hundreds of sensors and tags. Fortunately, a majority of the time (>99.99%) they indicate that no extraordinary event is occurring. Because there are time-series patterns present, they can be modeled and used to detect when there is a deviation from the normal pattern. Determining these models allows Duke to look forward with a very short-term forecast and then instantly detect an event of interest.

Event Identification

Once you've detected an event, you have to identify the type of event. An event of interest doesn't necessarily mean there is a problem or that one will develop. Some events are random, like a lightning strike or a tree hitting a power line, while others represent some type of equipment failure. Duke has determined that many of these events produce a similar signature in the data stream because time-series-similarity analysis and time-series clustering have been able to match the incoming events to previously seen events. Knowing which previous event signatures are non-consequential allows them to safely ignore them. Figures 24.3 and 24.4 show how similarity analysis is used for event identification.

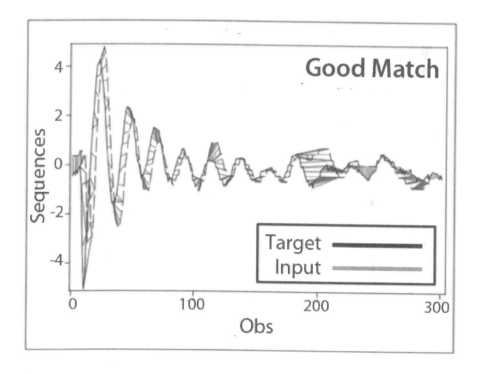

Figure 24.3 Similarity analysis – Good match

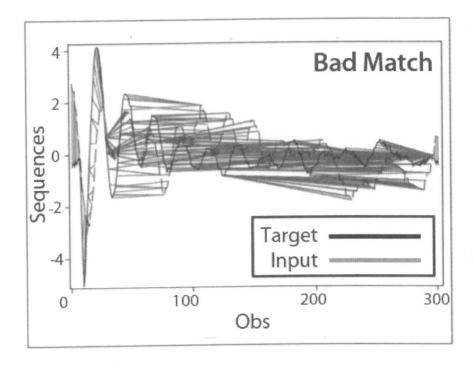

Figure 24.4 Similarity analysis – Bad match

Event Quantification

For some events, the question is if the magnitude of the event gives cause for concern. An example is oscillation on the power grid. Small but diminishing oscillations are not necessarily a problem, but larger ones that are increasing may require further attention. Once the event type is identified, each has some specialized techniques to determine their magnitude and consequence.

Do

Voltage stability is a growing concern for most large power systems and the challenges of providing a reliable power service are only increasing. Reliability of power varies significantly across the globe. For example, the U.S. has an average of nine hours of disruptions each year for every consumer; those interruptions are estimated to result in economical losses of least $150B annually. Compared to other industrialized countries, the reliability of the U.S. grid is 5–10 times less than in major European countries. The average electricity consumer in the U.S. has to cope with approximately 30 times more service interruptions each year than in Japan or Singapore.[5]

Duke Energy's work shows the potential of using data to predict problems in time for operators to respond and in doing so, deliver precision power.

---

[5]https://www.allianz.com/v_1339677769000/media/responsibility/documents/
position_paper_power_blackout_risks.pdf

25

Precision Farming

August Farms is located in the Cotswolds area of England. Owned and operated by Nick August, the farm has been in his family for more than 70 years and currently yields wheat, rapeseed and peas on 1,235 acres. You'll probably find very few farmers who can talk about serial interfaces and HTML and even fewer trying to use a vast array machines and sensors to improve crop yield and quality like Nick; however, he's quick to point out that "precision farming won't make a good farmer out of a bad farmer."

In this case, you'll see both examples of machine data and nomic (in this case agronomic) data. This pattern also appears in industries like healthcare, where machine manufacturers build gene sequencers, MRIs and blood analyzers. There is both data about the machines as well as nomic data coming from the machines, such as blood oxygen levels of gene sequences. AGCO has discussed its two-pipe strategy as a means of segregating the two types of data for agricultural machines.

This case will also illustrate the complexity of using multiple machines from multiple generations of technology and multiple sensors to enable the delivery of precision farming products.

Things

Nick operates several machines including a seed drill, solid fertilizer broadcast spreader, liquid sprayer, and combine to plant, fertilize, protect and harvest his crop.

Seed Drill
A seed drill precisely positions seeds in the soil and then covers them. It makes a small burrow (about the size of your finger) and then deposits the seeds at equal distances and a specific depth, ensuring that the seeds get covered with soil, which fosters good germination and provides protection from birds.

Nick's seed drill is an eight-meter wide Väderstad SeedHawk. The Väderstad is interfaced to a Topcon X30 — a console with multi-view interface. At August Farms this serves as the automated control. The Topcon X30 uploads what are called *prescription maps*; farmers create these maps by uploading soil-type data, historical-yield data and aerial imagery into farm management software.

Figure 25.1 Väderstad SeedHawk Seed Drill

In Nick's case, formulas within Trimble's Farm Works farm management software are used to calculate prescription maps using weights for each criterion. Jobs are prepared in advance for different possible scenarios, like dry or wet planting and early or late season. Export files are created in SHP (developed by Environmental Systems Research Institute) or XML format, and exported for use in the Topcon X30.

Solid Fertilizer Broadcast Spreader
The basic operating concept of the broadcast fertilizer spreader is simple. A large hopper is positioned over a horizontal spinning disk with a series of fins attached that throw the fertilizer from the hopper out and away from the spreader. Nick uses a Kuhn MDS 1141, which you can see attached to the tractor in Figure 25.2.

Figure 25.2 Kuhn Solid Fertilizer Spreader

You can control how far the fertilizer goes by varying the aperture, disk speed and angulations. The Kuhn has a legacy LH Agro 5000 connection, which Nick interfaced to the Topcon X30 to control the spreader.

A number of activities occur with regards to the fertilizer spreader. Rate of flow is calibrated for each fertilizer (e.g., urea or ammonium nitrate); sensors measure the opening of the aperture; spreading width is entered into the onboard computer; and forward speed is taken from GPS. With this information, among other things, fluctuations in forward speed and prescription rates can now be accounted for. Accuracy of rate governance is better that 95%, with 98% commonly achieved. Product density and shape, wind and humidity have a significant influence on how the product spreads, with a variance of 6–10% over the spreading width considered acceptable.

The spreader sends applied rate and engaged information back to the Topcon X30 for recording purposes. In the near future, data from the Topcon X30 will be remotely collected either by GPRS (a data service on 2G or 3G cellular networks), WiFi or cell phone. Today the data is sent to a USB thumb drive.

Liquid Sprayer

The sprayer, which sprays liquid fertilizer, herbicides, fungicides and pesticides, is a self-propelled, Multidrive 6185 with a Chafer 24-meter contractor boom and 4,000-liter spray pack.

Figure 25.3 Liquid Sprayer

The sprayer also uses the Topcon X30 as an interface, with similar attributes as when used with a solid product spreader. The Topcon X30 will send and record application rates, user and machine settings to a USB thumb drive and controls sections, spray pump settings and nozzle selection. At August Farms, automated systems for regulating the rate of fertilizer application have generally performed below expectation, with little or no net improvement in optimal fertilizer use. It has recently become understood that wide row spacing (the norm in the U.S. is 250mm; the norm in the UK is 125mm) has a detrimental effect on crop sensors, with those that look directly downward especially affected.

Combine Harvester

The combine harvester (or simply combine) is a machine that harvests grain crops. The name is derived from its combining of three separate operations — reaping, threshing and winnowing — into a single process. Nick's combine is a Massey Ferguson MF 7382.

It is connected thru AgCommand, which is AGCO's telemetry tool and one of the key enabling technologies powering its Fuse Connected Services. AgCommand is available at two levels of service. Level 1 is self-monitoring and Level 2 connects the dealer. AgCommand transmits at five-second intervals while the local system, Taskdoc, records every second.

Data recorded on the combine harvester falls into two categories: Machine data, which helps to manage the machine and its efficiency, and agronomic data for crop management. The machine data is everything from engine temperature and fuel level to monitoring shaft speeds and grain losses. For crop management, yield and moisture are recorded on a spatial basis and communicated to the farm office via GPRS mobile phone signal and Bluetooth when in range of a receiver.

The combine also has Topcon auto guidance to help the operator maximize the machine capacity and reduce fatigue. New software will link the screen to optical sensing technology to monitor, display and record grain yield alongside moisture content, speed, area, work rate and harvest-rate monitors to give real-time yield and moisture maps.

Crop maturity and weather dictate the timing of harvest. Once a crop is ripe such that the moisture is below about 16% for wheat, barley and peas and 9% for rapeseed, it is fit to harvest. After that, the crop is vulnerable to weather events, which brings us to a set of agronomic sensors that Nick uses.

Agronomic Sensors

There are several other pieces of equipment in the field that provide more data about the crops. These include Zeltex for protein content, Holland Scientific for crop-canopy sensor, SOYLsense LAI for satellite images and Yara N-Tester for nitrogen testing.

Protein content is also recorded with a Zeltex AccuHarvest and is logged onto an SD card. As you harvest, the AccuHarvest samples the grain four to five times per minute. The AccuHarvest's optics and sampling technique provides fast and accurate analysis of protein, moisture and oil. This information is logged by a DataLogger, which displays the current reading and a bin average, and can be used later to create accurate field maps.

Nick uses Holland Scientific's Crop Circle ACS-430 active-crop canopy sensor. The Crop Circle provides vegetation index data and basic reflectance information from plant canopies and soil. Most systems record near infrared light and other wavelengths to calculate a normalized difference vegetation index (NDVI), leaf area index (LAI) or green area index (GAI). The sensor is used as a stand-alone unit, recording the information and sending it back to the farm office on an SD card. The data is then merged with yield expectation for each zone and a prescription map is created. Because of the problems associated with wide rows, sensors that scan across the crop are being investigated.

For satellite-based data, Nick uses SOYLsense LAI, whose scans allow the subscriber to identify and manage variations in crop-canopy development. Regular satellite passes ensure frequent collection of satellite imagery. SOYLsense works closely with a range of satellite providers to ensure maximum imagery availability. The satellite sensors measure light reflected from the crop canopy. A thicker, healthier crop can be distinguished from bare soil or a thinner crop because of differences in the reflectance characteristics, which are shown in the raw satellite data.

For nitrogen, Nick uses the N-Min test, which predicts the fertilizer requirement for various crops; Nick uses crop sensors on only a small proportion of the crop, but N-Min tests have become important to predict how much extra nitrogen a crop might need to achieve a predicted yield. Extra nitrogen may be required to meet quality specifications of a target market.

Connect

The combine is connected via cellular and by Bluetooth to a laptop. None of the other equipment is connected, but it's expected that the Topcon X30 will connect to a Topcon cloud soon. Today, with sneaker networking (e.g., USB drive or SD cards), all the data is collected into Trimble's Farm Works. The Topcon X30 controller is physically transferred to the tractor to control a Kuhn MDS 1141 solid fertilizer spreader, Tive 6260 pneumatic spreader or the Multidrive 6185 liquid sprayer.

Collect

All data from sensors is collected on a PC in Nick's office using Trimble's Farm Works desktop software, which uses information gathered during the growing season to help make smarter management decisions. Data can be imported from most precision farming displays or entered manually. Soil types, yield maps and other data are used in creating simple, variable-rate prescription maps. The software allows Nick to view and print product summaries to see total quantity needed to complete a job as well as the approximate cost.

Learn

Nick divides fields into a series of different zones to create individual prescriptions across the farm. With the help of Andrew Richards from Masstock and Randy Wilbrink of Consilion Technologies, Nick has been looking at yield maps, aerial images and historical SOYLsense LAI scans and confirming (aka: ground truthing) this information by digging soil pits.

The maps make it simple to monitor crop development and form a base for nitrogen decision-making. Whole-farm maps are also created to aid further decision-making. Nick and his agronomists make geo-referenced observations while *crop walking* on their Connected Farm application, which connects back to the office via cellular.

Nick combines this information with the Crop Circle results and local knowledge to predict the output potential from each zone, treating each zone separately, although some may have the same treatments while others differ.

Do

Precision farming has the potential to lower the cost of consumables (fuel, fertilizer, pesticides) as well as improve the quality of the end product. Controlled traffic farming (CTF) is a management tool used to reduce the damage to soils caused by heavy or repeated agricultural machinery passes on the land; it is a system that confines all machinery loads to the least possible area of permanent traffic lanes and makes use of all of the precision-farming hardware. As all the machines are auto-guided across the field at sub-2cm accuracy and on the same A-B line, the field is worked in the most efficient way and the machine has no skips or overlaps. Using

CTF and no-till crop establishment, fuel consumption can be reduced from 60 to 5.9 liters per hectare for crop establishment.

For the crops themselves, the potential is to dramatically improve productivity, reduce impact on the environment and use less to grow more. Today, there might be a 3–5% savings in consumables (fertilizer, fuel, seed) to achieve the same level of crop productivity, but according to Nick, it's hardly worth the current investment.

As you can tell, precision farming today is a complex data integration problem, perhaps as complicated as any enterprise challenge. There is conflicting scientific information on various aspects of fertilizer management and the creation of prescription maps is still in its infancy.

26

Precision Water

If you're like me, when you turn on the tap, you have little idea how the water got there. Living in California during the longest drought on record certainly raises your consciousness, but it wasn't until I spent time with Adam Setzler at McCrometer that I began to learn more. McCrometer started in California in the 1950s, predating any Silicon Valley startup. They designed, built and sold robust and reliable mechanical flow meters, which became a standard in the industry.

Water we drink or use for agriculture is either ground water or surface water. Ground water is the water we pump from underground and surface water is sourced from rivers, canals, or reservoirs. Some who live in Silicon Valley or San Francisco source their drinking water from the Hetch Hetchy Reservoir, which collects snow melt from the Sierras and is then brought here through a series of pipes and canals. Midwestern states like Nebraska sit on top of the Ogallala

Aquifer, which is one of the world's most productive aquifers. And those on the east coast — where it rains much more than in the west — depend more on surface water.

Water is managed in many different ways across the United States. Some areas have created public — and others, private — water utility companies. In my own area, Purissima Hills Water District serves approximately 6,400 residents and 10 institutional customers. An elected board of directors governs the district. A general manager oversees district operations performed by a two-person office staff, a part-time conservation coordinator and a five-person field crew.

In the early 1950s, there were several hundred homes and small ranches in an area west of Los Altos. Some residents had private wells while others had organized themselves into small, mutual water associations, which distributed water obtained from community wells. There was a drought in 1952 and in response to the water shortage, a group of citizens formed the Purissima Hills Water District. The original water system included two 100,000-gallon redwood tanks. Water was delivered to the lower tank via a pipeline from the Hetch Hetchy pipes. Today, the district has eleven tanks and a storage capacity of almost 10 million gallons.

Water utilities have a variety of reasons to be interested in measuring water flow. Some do it purely for accounting purposes, and others from a water management and conservation point of view. Similarly, large consumers of water (e.g., farmers) will instrument their water usage; some because they are required to by law, and some because they are managing water just as they are precisely managing their fertilizer and pesticide usage.

Things

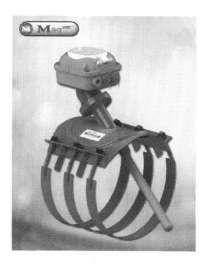

Figure 26.1 Mc Mag 3000 Flow Meter

For this case, we'll discuss a couple of sensors that McCrometer sells, including water-flow meters, weather stations and soil-moisture meters. Water-flow meters such as the Mc Mag 3000 use electromagnetic technology to measure water flow. The sensor corrects for shifting velocity in the pipe by constantly obtaining the mean velocity from multiple electrodes. The Mc Mag 3000 is packaged with field-replaceable batteries and designed for a five-year operation in the field, selling for around $2,000.

Figure 26.2 Weather Station

Shown in Figure 26.2, the A753 addWAVE weather station can report rainfall, temperature, relative humidity, wind speed, wind direction, solar radiation, leaf wetness, soil temperature, wet-bulb temperature and dew-point temperatures. This data may be used in models to estimate crop water demand, disease or pest risk, development stages of the crop, or frost risk.

McCrometer also provides soil-moisture sensors, which can operate as single-point sensors or multi-depth probes. Most soil-moisture-sensor data is in units of "percent volume of water," representing the proportion of soil volume occupied by water (as opposed to air or soil). Also common are units of soil water tension, which can be thought of as the suction required to remove water from the soil. Many soil-moisture sensors may also provide soil temperature and salinity, which can assist farmers with planting, irrigation, and fertilizer application decisions.

Connect

McCrometer provides wireless connection for all of these devices. There is both an Ultra-High Frequency (UHF) radio and General Packet Radio Service (GPRS) cellular option. In the U.S., a band between 460–470 MHz has been allocated for UHF radio communication. A farm or water district can purchase a license for a portion of this spectrum from the FCC good for 10 years and covering a 20-mile radius. McCrometer's UHF radios are capable of reaching between 1–12 miles, depending on the RTU model and local terrain. McCrometer supplies a communication gateway that manages the network. The communication gateway is an Intel server running a version of the Linux operating system. A large-scale farm or water district might connect several hundred to thousands of meters.

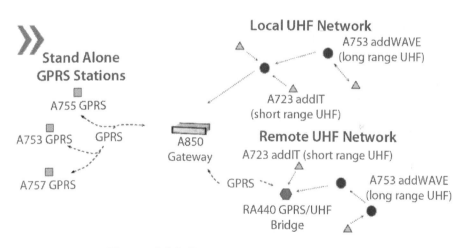

Figure 26.3 Connection Architecture

A GPRS option is also available. In this case, AT&T, US Cellular and T-Mobile will provide a cellular network connection and management with a SIM card — like you have on your cell phone — added to each of the RTUs. Data can be transmitted on a flexible schedule, but 15-minute intervals are common. Monthly data plans range from \$5–50 per month, depending on sensors connected and data frequency. For remote locations, there is also the ability to use satellite transmission, although this will typically limit data updates.

The raw data is in a proprietary protocol and is not human readable. A simple authentication code is used to pair each of the meters with the gateway so that one water district or farmer will not deliberately or accidently receive data from meters that are not their own.

Collect

Data is collected from the flow meters at a rate that can vary from one sample per minute down to once per day, which is used when satellite connections are implemented. Data being transmitted every 15 minutes is the most common interval. Interestingly, weather station data is also available at this frequency.

The RTUs connected to the meters have the capability to store data and standard models can hold up to six months' worth of information at 15-minute intervals. In some applications, this can be important for reporting purposes. If communications are lost (i.e. someone knocks over an RTU or a cell tower goes down), any missed historical data will be transmitted when communications are restored.

The communication gateways have some storage as well, but ultimately the data is pulled into centralized storage. McCrometer and some of its dealers provide a service to store the data, although some government clients prefer to use their own infrastructure. The centralized collection management is based on HyperSQL running on Microsoft Windows. Gateways are typically polled for new data every fifteen minutes.

It's fairly common for a water district to have 2,000 meters, with larger water districts having thousands of meters or more. For instance, one of the Nebraska natural resource districts has over 20,000 irrigation wells. On the farming side, the average number of meters managed by a typical grower is less than irrigation districts, but can still reach a few hundred or even more than a thousand meters. For example, a large pistachio farmer in California has nearly 1,500 meters.

One of McCrometer's larger in-house production servers, which services about 100 customers, has 500 meters connected and has been running since 2012. This server has collected roughly 600 million data points and is nearing 50GB in size.

Learn

So what is done with the data? Some of their customers are using the data to identify when an irrigation system is malfunctioning or not operating efficiently. As an example, the combination of flow rate and pressure data can provide a simple diagnostic for system operation. High pressure with very low or no flow can indicate an obstruction in the line, clogged filter, closed valve, or a malfunctioning meter. Flow with little or no pressure may indicate a leak in the line. Trends of flow rate and pressure over time may also indicate when pump performance is degrading (from maintenance issues or reduction in water supply).

Data is also being used to create ground and surface water models. Some natural resource districts in Nebraska have built models of local groundwater and surface water resources. While groundwater is a renewable source of water, reserves may replenish relatively slowly. The model attempts to predict the amount of water coming into and leaving the aquifer, and therefore, the future state.

Precision farmers are also using data for irrigation management. As a homeowner with a lawn, you can appreciate that if you knew how much water your lawn needed, how much is being lost through evaporation, transpiration (water absorbed through the grass), and how much rain you got today, you could have computers control your sprinklers for precision watering.

Using a dataset of soil moisture time-series collected over several months (or years) from multiple probes across multiple sites, McCrometer would like to learn how to forecast future soil moisture readings from the time-series of past readings. The aim is to be able to forecast future soil moisture values up to 7–10 days out. With this information, the farmer (or wine grower, etc.) can then plan their watering schedule to ensure that the soil maintains an optimal moisture level. In addition, evaporation data from weather stations can be integrated into the forecasting model to improve the accuracy of the predictions. In this way, soil watering can be optimized to ensure that the right amount of water is applied at the right time.

Do

Bethel Farms grows turf and citrus on about 4,000 acres near Arcadia, Florida. In 2009 they installed the McCrometer system; it includes multiple locations measuring flow, soil moisture, salinity, conductivity, solar radiation, soil and ambient temperature, humidity, wind speed and direction.

All of this data goes via GPRS to their office's server, which takes all the information and translates it into a report. Some of that data, like rainfall and irrigation cycles, is fed into the Farm Works application. Between some infrastructure changes and their instrumentation, they are reducing groundwater withdraws by 35%. The IoT application also sends alerts for frosts, freezes and wind, and implements disease prediction, which is based on measuring the disease triangle — the host, disease and environment. All three have to line up to have a disease outbreak. By monitoring the environment and the host you can identify points where the disease is at higher risk. Given that information, you move from a schedule-based pesticide-spraying cycle to a spray-on-demand cycle, which of course reduces costs in pesticide and labor. Furthermore, by applying pesticides as needed, the diseases do not develop pesticide resistance as frequently.

One event at Bethel Farms has paid for investment in the application. One season, they were able to predict a rhizoctonia large patch outbreak in their Empire Zoysia turf and apply a protective and softer fungicide application. They also created a control area and within two weeks it looked like "martians had landed on it." The protective application was about $100 per acre, while it cost $300 per acre to clean up the control area. On a 158-acre field, avoiding a cost of $300 per acre paid for the IoT application.

27

Precision Cooling Tower

If you like Shakespeare's *Much Ado About Nothing* and live near Seattle, you may have seen Max Martina playing the part of Don Pedro. You might be surprised to learn that Max is also the President at Griswold Water Systems (GWS). GWS has much ado with helping us conserve water and protect health and human safety by enhancing water treatment to support cooling tower operations.

Cooling towers have been around since the industrial revolution and work by lowering water temperature through evaporation. This efficient endothermic process mimics perspiration in the human body when moisture helps dissipate heat. Water-cooled processes are usually preferred over air-cooled processes because water conducts heat more effectively, which is why cooling towers can be found the world over.

What's astonishing is that a single, modestly sized cooling tower can consume millions of gallons of water annually. Additionally, the warm, moist environment of a cooling tower can breed harmful bacteria, including the type that causes Legionellosis (Legionnaires' disease). Actually, this disease is named after the 1976 American Legion convention in Philadelphia where 221 people were affected and 34 later died.[6] The source was a contaminated water tower in the hotel's cooling system. In addition to the health risk, untreated water can also form scale (calcium deposits) that can clog pipes, waste energy, and lead to system fouling. By one measure, system fouling in heat transfer equipment negatively impacts U.S. GDP by 0.25%.[7]

---

[6] http://www.thelegionnaireslawyer.com/history-legionnaires-disease/
[7] H. Mueller-Steinhagen, M.R. Malayeri and A.P. Watkinson, "Fouling of Heat Exchanger--New Approaches to Solve Old Problem", Heat Transfer Engineering, 26(2), 2005

To combat these threats, the industry has traditionally relied on chemical service providers to treat the water on a monthly basis with toxic chemicals, such as biocides, algaecides, and various scale and corrosion inhibitors. These chemicals are designed to prevent biological contamination and eliminate system fouling.

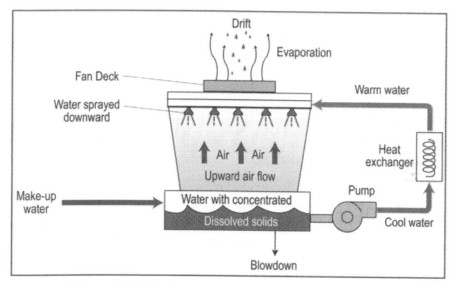

Figure 27.1 Typical Cooling Tower Architecture

The use of chemicals to treat cooling-tower water presents two fundamental challenges. First, a lot of water is wasted; much of the water must be discharged to the sewer because the now toxic water cannot be sent to landscape irrigation or down the storm drain. The result can be astronomical sewage fees.

Second, if there is a dosing system or tower component malfunction, the water chemistry can become unbalanced, often leading to bacterial outbreaks or system-wide scaling, which can threaten human safety and shut down the equipment.

Monthly service visits don't always discover these problems because system hiccups often occur between chemical service visits. This has led to an industry plagued by system fouling, high turnover among chemical services firms, and the frustration of cooling system operators with little recourse but to perpetually fire and replace the chemical services firms.

GWS, with its partners Autodesk and Hollis Controls, believed there was a better way and took a new approach to cooling towers: treat the water with electric fields instead of chemicals. This allows, on average, the conservation of up to 28% of total tower-water consumption and can amount to millions of gallons of water saved annually. For instance, the water discharged from the cooling tower—now free from chemicals—can be used onsite, obviating the need for additional water purchase. Finally, a remote monitoring solution is deployed to continuously monitor the system and allow for rapid deployment of human service if a problem in the system occurs.

Things

GWS equipment accomplishes biological control through a process called *electroporation*, whereby bacteria are injured by a strong electric field and cannot reproduce. As injured bacteria are flushed from the system, there's less organic matter to support biofilm—colonies of bacteria that pose a distinct health risk. When GWS equipment is deployed, biofilm is eliminated and biological counts often hover close to drinking water standards.

Modulating electric fields also precipitate calcium that was previously dissolved in the water. The GWS approach to using electric fields gets a boost by incorporating a filtration system that removes the precipitated solids—and other blown-in debris—from the system, which enhances overall system cleanliness.

Perhaps where the GWS approach gains even more significant traction with customers is its ability to monitor essential cooling tower operating data. To do so, GWS uses a Netduino open-source single-board processor running the STMicro STM32F4 microcontroller and the .NET Micro Framework 4.3. In addition, sensors are added to measure:

- Water flow. When water is flowing, stagnant water is avoided and all parts of the cooling system receive treated water. This also ensures GWS equipment can effectively treat passing bacteria.
- GWS equipment performance. If GWS equipment isn't emitting proper signal or if its treatment module is turned off, the cooling system will have no treatment. GWS effectively eliminates "the lack of water treatment" from the customer's sphere of risk.
- Water conductivity measured in microsiemens/centimeter. Cooling systems use a conductivity meter to measure the amount of dissolved solids in the water. Knowing this setpoint is crucial to water efficiency and essential to controlling corrosion.

The Netduino board runs in a continuous loop, monitoring the sensors at one-second intervals.

Connect

Data is transmitted over a 3G wireless connection via a Maestro M100 series modem on the cooling tower—an essential requirement given that most cooling towers are on rooftops or removed from easy Ethernet connectivity. To create a complete solution, GWS uses Wyless—a worldwide mobile operator—to connect the cooling towers. Wyless has partnered with 20 carriers and hundreds of networks worldwide to provide coverage, whether the water tower is deployed in a remote area or in the middle of a large city.

At the application layer, GWS uses Autodesk's Fusion Connect. The Netduino protocols, as well as the Wyless API for providing device connection statistics, were selected from Fusion Connect's library of plug-in devices and partner services.

Collect

Autodesk's Fusion Connect runs on Amazon's compute and storage cloud service. Data is stored in a SQL Postgres and NoSQL Cassandra database infrastructure. In addition, the service is highly available across many servers and backed up daily.

Learn

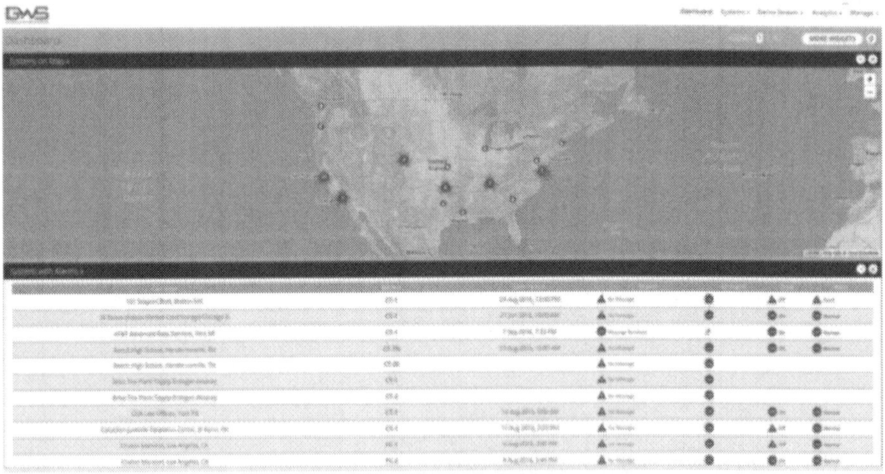

Figure 27.2 Fusion Connect Dashboard Example

The Fusion Connect platform includes a data analyzer, online dashboard, reporting tool and web-page builder, as shown in Figure 27.2. These tools enable the relevant stakeholders to configure views that quickly determine the status of a particular cooling tower, such as the last time it was heard from or if any faults have occurred. If a sensor detects a potential fault—such as a loss of power to the treatment unit, a disruption in water flow, or a breached conductivity setpoint—the unit determines whether to notify the building owner/operator, building maintenance person, and/or the company responsible for servicing the cooling tower.

Typically, the creation of such a connected product solution involves extensive programming or scripting skills, which can be hard to find, especially in house. In fact, the creation of the Netduino board and its connection to the Fusion Connect platform was outsourced to Hollis Controls and its president Tom Duff. Hollis Controls is a small company primarily involved with power supply design for the military and aviation markets. Tom and his team have decades of experience building such products, but have limited programming resources. Fortunately, the creation of a product model within the Fusion Connect platform requires zero programming because it's done through a sequence of dropdown menus. In fact, the Hollis Controls team was able to connect the Netduino board that they customized for GWS to the Autodesk platform in less than a week.

Do

So what's the benefit to a customer who uses GWS equipment to treat cooling towers?

In contrast to the GWS approach, it's worth noting that chemical treatment requires a never-ending consumable cost: the chemicals and the cost of labor to apply the chemicals. When using the GWS solution, no toxic chemicals are required and the on-site human service requirements are substantially reduced.

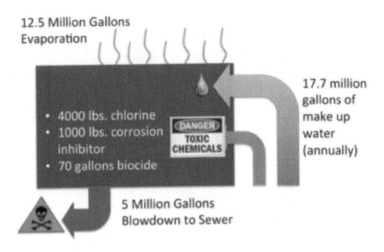

12.5 Million Gallons
Evaporation

- 4000 lbs. chlorine
- 1000 lbs. corrosion inhibitor
- 70 gallons biocide

DANGER
TOXIC
CHEMICALS

17.7 million gallons of make up water (annually)

5 Million Gallons
Blowdown to Sewer

Figure 27.3 Chemically Treated Cooling Tower Example

Not only does a precision cooling tower eliminate the need for chemicals, but it also reduces water usage. To put this into perspective, Figure 27.3 shows a sample 1,000-ton cooling tower running year-round; using chemical treatment in a traditional scenario, the cooling tower would use 17.7 million gallons of make-up water annually. In addition, five million gallons of now toxic water would need to be flushed down the sewer.

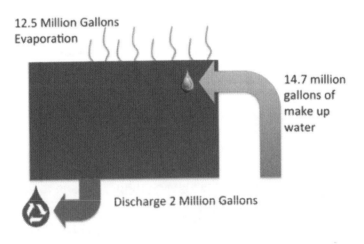

12.5 Million Gallons
Evaporation

14.7 million gallons of make up water

Discharge 2 Million Gallons

Figure 27.4 Precision Cooling Tower Example

Replacing chemical treatment with the GWS solution, as shown in Figure 27.4, allows the tower water to be more concentrated with dissolved solids. This can result in the reduction of three million gallons of make-up water annually, or 17%. The savings don't stop there. The two million gallons of discharged water is non-toxic; therefore, it can be reused for things like landscaping. Overall water consumption can be reduced further to 12.7 million gallons, representing a 28% overall water savings. To pin a conservative dollar amount to this savings, and using national average water and sewer costs, combined water and sewer charges will drop from $76,000 to $51,000 for a savings of $25,000 per year, or a rapid return on investment for the customer of less than 12 months.

Finally, by leveraging remote monitoring to collect and transmit essential water treatment data and tower operating parameters, GWS addresses a significant source of operator frustration, namely, the limitations of the traditional, monthly chemical dosing mechanism. Traditionally, because chemical dosing pumps and meters are more expensive to monitor and are therefore rarely employed, system hiccups in water treatment— such as stuck valves elsewhere in the system or an empty chemical feed tank—dramatically impact the performance and longevity of the tower. Thus, even though a chemical service partner may visit a facility once per month, a system disruption the day after a service visit will lead to cooling tower performance degradation if left unchecked until the following visit; this can result in widespread scaling or biological contamination within the tower.

In contrast, GWS is armed with the knowledge needed to dispatch a human service partner immediately should a fault be detected. Consequently, its solution reduces the average time cooling-tower-water chemistry spends out of calibration during a tower's estimated 15-year lifespan from 675 days to fewer than 90—a reduction of over 85%. The result is a tower that is more efficient, less expensive to operate, and significantly cleaner. Owners and operators thereby eliminate employee exposure to toxic chemicals, conserve precious resources, and reduce the very real risk of a legionella outbreak.

In fact, in a dirty system, these extremely dangerous biological life forms can escape as mist and be inhaled by anyone within two miles or more depending on atmospheric conditions. There are an estimated 8,000 to 18,000 cases of Legionnaires' disease per year in the United States that require hospitalization; there is no known vaccine and 10% of those infected die.[8] For instance, in July and August of 2015, an outbreak in the Bronx, NY killed twelve people and made about 120 people sick. The city found that bacteria had regrown in at least fifteen cooling towers under chemical treatment that had been disinfected just two months prior.[9]

In light of the tens of thousands of cooling towers currently operating in the United States, you might want to ask your own facility's team: how is the water in my office building's cooling tower treated... and could there be a better way?

---

[8] https://en.wikipedia.org/wiki/Legionnaires'_disease
[9] Legionnaires' Bacteria Regrew in Bronx Cooling Towers That Were Disinfected http://www.nytimes.com/2015/10/02/nyregion/legionnaires-bacteria-regrew-in-bronx-cooling-towers-that-were-disinfected.html

28

Precision Race Car

A few years ago I was introduced to track racing and have since had the opportunity to drive at Laguna Seca where I navigated the infamous Corkscrew—successfully. So when I heard Sam Schmidt's story, I was impressed, to say the least. Sam started racing professionally at the age of 31—which is relatively old compared to professional racing norms—and was named rookie of the year in 1995. Considered a rising star, Sam raced three consecutive times in the Indianapolis 500 and netted his first victory from the pole at the Las Vegas Motor Speedway in 1999.

In January 2000, Sam had a terrible crash during a practice lap at the Walt Disney World Speedway in Orlando, FL and was tragically paralyzed from the neck down. Sam's racing days were over, or so it seemed.

In 2013, Sam met with a group of engineers at Arrow Electronics Inc. and together they decided to set course with an ambitious goal: enable Sam to drive again. By 2014, Sam was speeding down the racetrack at more than 100 mph—driving all on his own. Read on to find out how.

Things

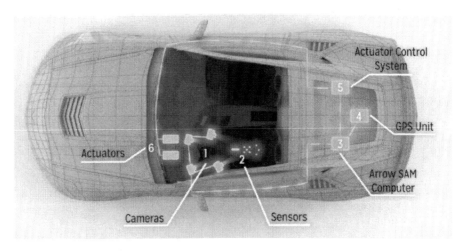

Figure 28.1 High Level SAM Car Architecture

In 2014, the engineering team at Arrow created the first version of a semi-autonomous motorcar they called the SAM Car. The current version of the SAM Car debuted in early 2016 and is a modified 2016 Corvette ZO6. The heart of the car's systems is the SAM Computer, which provides the gateway between a number of cameras and sensors, the actuator control system that controls the vehicle, and a GPS unit for precise, real-time monitoring of the car's physical location.

The SAM Computer gateway is from Advantech. It has been ruggedized for automotive applications and runs on an Intel Atom-based processor and the QNX operating system. It also runs the Arrow Connect gateway software.

The SAM Car's sensors pull data associated with both the car and the car's driver. The car data includes information on the car's performance, handling and speed, and the in-vehicle environment such as brightness, temperature and humidity. Sensors also gather data about the driver such as heart rate and body temperature.

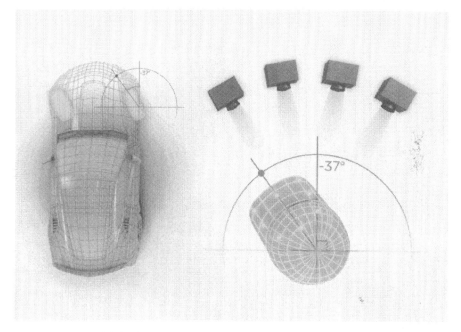

Figure 28.2 Sensors embedded into the driver's helmet

To handle steering, there are eight reflective, infrared sensors fitted into the driver's helmet (and more recently the helmet has been replaced with sunglasses), while four infrared cameras face the driver. To steer, the driver simply has to look in the direction he or she wants to go. For you track drivers, that would be the apex of the turn (usually marked with a bright orange cone for us rookies).

All input from the cameras and sensors integrate into a single camera PC, which connects to the SAM Computer to track the driver's head movements in real time. The camera PC uses an Intel i7 processor running Microsoft Windows 7. The system also deploys Motive software that tracks the rigid body markers on the driver's helmet or sunglasses and outputs the angle of the driver's head from the camera PC to the SAM Computer.

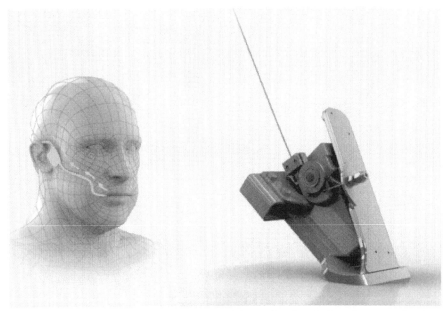

Figure 28.3 Acceleration and braking via the driver's mouthpiece

To handle acceleration, the driver puffs breaths of air into a mouthpiece equipped with an NXP pressure sensor, specifically selected to be sensitive enough to respond to the driver's breath input: the stronger the breath intensity, the stronger the acceleration rate. The car then responds directly via a rotary actuator attached to the gas pedal. The gas pedal is depressed based on the amount of air pressure the driver creates, giving him full control over acceleration, from a smooth gradual increase to the quick acceleration demanded in racing conditions.

Braking is accomplished through the same mouth-pressure sensor. The driver sips on the mouthpiece creating negative pressure that the system translates into braking. The driver can coast at a chosen speed by not continuing to sip or puff air after the desired speed is achieved.

The actual control of the car is handled by a Paravan drive system, which includes microprocessors that transmit signals in nanoseconds to one servomotor for the brake and accelerator and a rotary actuator on the steering wheel. Sensor and camera data processed by the SAM Computer are sent as messages over a controller area network to the Paravan system. The Paravan drive system sends updates 100 times per second (10 milliseconds) to the actuators, enabling real-time control of the car.

Connect

Through a GPS unit located onboard the vehicle, the SAM Computer connects outside of the car over a 4G LTE modem to the Arrow Connect Cloud.

One form of data transmitted is the vehicle's telemetry data, using TLS 1.2 for transport, AES-256 for data encryption and SHA-256 for data hashing. This data is used to keep the car within 1.5 meters from the inside edge of the racetrack wall. In essence, this GPS system establishes "visual curbs" or boundaries, as the car is programmed to act according to its GPS location. If the car gets too close to the wall, it warns the driver to correct course. If the car continues to drift toward the wall, the system gently auto-corrects the car to keep it safely on the track.

In addition, the car's sensor and video data are also transmitted. Sensor data is streamed in real-time—or stored and forwarded when in a disconnected state—and is transmitted using REST and MQTT protocols. Also, when high-speed Internet connectivity is available, the SAM Computer stores and forwards the video.

Collect

The Arrow Connect Cloud runs on the Microsoft Azure compute and storage cloud service and uses MongoDB as its underlying database. To date, the SAM Car has generated and stored more than five million records that include 1GB of sensor data and 3GB of videos. This data was generated from about one dozen races/events.

Learn

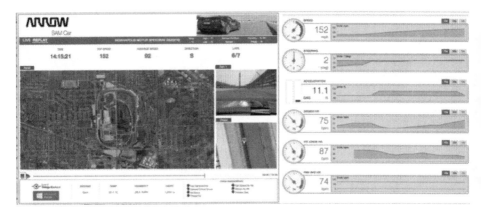

Figure 28.4 SAM Car Dashboard

The Arrow Connect Cloud offers an API to enable third-party applications to visualize, integrate and analyze the data coming from the SAM Car. For instance, as shown in Figure 28.4, Arrow created a dynamic visual dashboard to display the data collection for spectators, pit crew, engineering teams and anyone interested in reviewing the technical performance of the car. The display features vehicle data collected from the main systems, including speed (top speed, average speed), steering degrees and acceleration. The dashboard also displays information from the subsystems, including in-vehicle temperature, humidity and light, and elements of FMEA diagnostics data.

Do

Figure 28.5 Sam Schmidt

Remarkably, in May 2016, Sam achieved 152 mph in the SAM Car during practice laps at the Indianapolis 500. And in June 2016, he completed the Broadmoor Pikes Peak International Hill Climb in Colorado, famed for its 4,725 ft. elevation gain and 156 hairpin turns and twists over the 12.42 mile course, managing to reach 80 mph on some straightaways.

29

Solutions Summary

If you've been in Silicon Valley in the past several years you've probably heard the phrase coined by Marc Andreessen, "Software is eating the world," which could now be amended to say, "Software and data are eating the world." As a manufacturer of any industrial or enterprise Thing (machine, asset, device), you'd be wise to listen to this phrase. Companies like GE and Bosch have already embraced this view and started investing significant amounts of money in the ability to connect, collect and learn from their machines. In the last several chapters, you've seen examples of what manufacturers of machines are doing and how it's beginning to change their business models. In time, it might be difficult to see the difference between a software company and a machine company.

So as a builder of enterprise Things, what are some of the steps to begin the digital transformation of your business?

First, you have to invest. That doesn't just mean buy software from a supplier and have them implement it; instead, you must invest in the talent. I did a talk for some of the senior managers at GE titled, *What's the Difference between Hardware and Software?* I highlighted two differences. With hardware, people tend to think that having a larger team to build a jet engine, for example, is better than having a smaller team. In software it's the opposite. I illustrated this idea with a story of a meeting with Oracle's Larry Ellison, Safra Catz and Jeff Henley. During the meeting, Jeff — who at that point was CFO — using a few salty expletives, asked Larry, "Why is the Salesforce.com' CRM product so much better when we have 500 developers and they only have 50?" Larry replied, "That's precisely the answer." Your investment in talent does not have to be 50 or 500, but you should at least start with the *right* five.

Of course, you're also going to invest in building machines with more sensors, more local computing and flexible communications. Consider the framework we've outlined in these books and think through what your high- and low-level connection architecture is going to be. How will you collect the data? What approaches will you use to learn from that data? How much will you buy? How much will you build? Should you sole-source with one supplier or build a stack unique to your business?

Again, what you've done is necessary but not sufficient. All of this technology is meaningless without answering how you're going to apply it and what the business benefit is. In previous chapters we discussed three major business models for the manufacturer of a wind turbine, blood analyzer and locomotive. First, connect the machine and provide a service contract. When Jack Welch was at the helm, GE made a major shift to this model; it's worked for them and also helped build some of the largest software companies.

Second, if you're connected to the combine, seed drill or fertilizer sprayer, you can also provide assisted services. Because you know what's happening on the equipment and, more importantly, have seen what works across hundreds or thousands of similar machines, you can advise on which could optimize performance, availability and security. And of course, if you can provide advice, you can also implement those changes and begin to offer machines-as-a-service and move to a highly profitable, recurring-revenue model.

There are challenges to doing this, least of which is being held hostage to the past. While many machines and devices have software, it has always been a necessary evil to the main player on the stage — the hardware. The November 2015 issue of the Economist said, "[…] the principal sticking-point in making this digital leap is often cultural […]."

As a machine manufacturer, integrating machine people with software people is not an easy task. Machine people focus on physical products and think about development lifecycles of three to five years; they know that after the start of production there's no stopping it and what is produced has to be deployed in the field and support a lifecycle of decades. On the other hand, the software people are thinking about minimum viable product, perpetual beta and updating your services daily. As a start, you might follow what GE has done in naming their chief digital officer, a person with equal executive footing to the leaders of GE Power, Aviation, etc.

The opportunities are large for both existing players and new entrants. As the role of software and analytic technology grows, the potential exists to build the next generation of machine in a totally different way. You don't need to look any farther than the car you drive to wonder if your next one will be from Ford or Apple.

Service Economy

Estimates vary, but 85–90% of the U.S. economy is a service economy. While a much lower percentage, Mexico and China are moving more and more toward becoming service economies. So what is a service economy? Officially, it includes every company that is not making something (manufacturing) or growing something (agriculture). The service economy includes industries like healthcare, retail, financial services, education, transportation and utilities.

So what is service? Is service answering the phone nicely from Bangalore? Is it flipping burgers at McDonald's? The simple answer is *no*. Service is the delivery of information that is personal and relevant to you; that could be the hotel concierge telling you where the best Szechwan Chinese restaurant in walking distance is, or your doctor telling you that based on your genome and lifestyle you should be on Lipitor. Service is precise information.

So if you're thinking about a future hospital, railway or farm, how should you think about your own digital transformation to delivering precision healthcare, transportation or agriculture?

Digital Transformation
If service is precise information, then start with finding all of it and making it personal and relevant to people. In a children's hospital, that would be the doctors, nurses, patients and parents. I implore you to not be held hostage by the SQL monster, but what does that mean?

Let's say it's the late 1990s; I have a bunch of SQL engineers in a room and I present them with a brilliant business idea. We are going to index the consumer Internet and we're going to monetize it with ads — we're going to be billionaires! Just guess what the SQL engineers would do?

The first thing they will do is design a master, global-data schema to index all the information on the planet. Then they will write ETL and data-cleansing tools to import all that information into this master schema. Finally, they are going to write reports on, for instance, the best place to camp in France or great places to eat in San Francisco.

If you are remotely technical you are probably laughing right now and thinking how completely idiotic that is. But I will contend that every city and business out there continues to try to adopt this mechanism to deliver any kind of information that might be personal and relevant.

Therefore, I would counsel you to consider that the term *consumerization of IT* does not apply to the question of whether or not you should use Facebook at work; instead, it speaks to the question of how to leverage these technologies to deliver personal and relevant information to the farmer, surgeon or power-plant operator?

Next, buy and connect smart machines. Whether that's a generator, blood analyzer or fertilizer sprayer — connect them. Allow the machine data to be used by the manufacturers to assist or implement higher performance, availability or security of the machines. The manufacturer is building precision machines because they are leveraging software and data across hundreds or hundreds of thousands of machines. Precision machines deliver higher quality service, lower cost consumables (e.g., fuel, fertilizer, ink) and lower cost of servicing the machines. As the farm, hospital or water plant of the future leverages these precision machines, you (as a service provider) will derive the benefits.

Furthermore, gather the nomic data, whether that's genomic or agronomic information. Again, applying the idea of connecting, collecting and learning from the nomic data will aid in delivering more precise pediatric care or more precise crops.

Challenges

The Internet of Things heightens existing concerns about cyber security and introduces new risks, multiplying the normal risks associated with any data communication. Each device increases the "surface area" available for breaches and interoperability expands their potential scope. Every node is a potential entry point and interconnection can spread the damage. Moreover, the consequences of compromised IoT systems that control the physical world could be catastrophic. A compromised medical monitor could be a matter or life or death. A hacker attack on a smart-grid system could potentially turn off power to millions of households and businesses, creating massive economic harm and threats to health and safety. Again, we're going to need to invest in innovative ways to protect these systems and engineer it into the products.

Finally, any digital transformation of an airline, hospital or mine will require people. We've already quoted the Economist, as well as highlighted how the biggest inhibitor will be the organization itself. In the end, leadership will be essential. Perhaps others will follow examples like the Children's Hospital of Orange County (CHOC), whose chief of pediatric cardiology has become the chief intelligence and innovation officer. Anthony Chang, while head of pediatric cardiology at CHOC, completed a master's degree in bioinformatics at Stanford.

Finally, as our population grows and we put more demands on the physical world, we're going to need to move toward becoming a precision planet; it makes no sense to waste water, fertilizer, pharmaceuticals and energy. It is widely recognized that global growth opportunities for the next several decades will be in Latin America, Southeast Asia and Africa. Africa is expected to account for more than half of the world's population growth between 2015 and 2050, according to the UN DESA report titled, *World Population Prospects: The 2015 Revision*. The population of Nigeria is projected to surpass that of the U.S. by about 2050, at which point it would become the third most populous country in the world.

Developing economies need infrastructure: power, water, agriculture, transportation, construction, healthcare and telecommunications. Will this infrastructure be built the 20th century way? Or, as we've seen in China, will developing economies leapfrog and move to 21st century cellular technology and never use 20th century landlines?

Africa may hold the keys to our next evolution. In the U.S., electric power is generated in large oil or coal-fired plants and distributed in a hierarchical manner. But in the modern world, you'd never do it that way; you'd take advantage of solar, wind and hydroelectric generation, all geographically distributed. Furthermore, you'd build some storage mechanisms, which our traditional power grids don't have. Essentially, the entire control of this power grid would be distributed and enabled by computers that have access to not only information about the wind turbine (generated every six seconds), but also the current weather and demand. And you may even move to generating direct current (DC) without ever going to alternating current (AC), as even lighting is moving to DC. In short, this future power system would look nothing like what we have today.

Building this in the U.S. today would be nearly impossible. In Africa, it would be the only way; you'd skip telephone lines and move directly to cellular. Africa holds the potential of skipping ahead to the next-generation farm, water treatment plant or hospital, unencumbered by the infrastructure and rules of the past. Perhaps you will become part of this evolution and redesign power, water, agriculture, education or healthcare for the planet. I certainly hope so.

Glossary of Terms

19-foot scissor lift – A sustainable option for your raised platform needs

3G – Short form of *third generation*; is the third generation of mobile telecommunications technology

A gene or DNA sequencer – An instrument used to determine the sequence or order of the four bases — G (guanine), C (cytosine), A (adenine) and T (thymine) — from any plant or animal cell

Accelerometer – An instrument for measuring acceleration, typically that of an automobile, ship, aircraft or spacecraft, or that involved in the vibration of a machine, building or other structure

ACID – Atomicity, Consistency, Isolation, Durability: a set of properties that guarantee that database transactions are processed reliably. In the context of databases, a single logical operation on the data is called a transaction

ACM – AGCO Connectivity Module

Advanced Encryption Standard – A symmetric block cipher used by the U.S. government to protect classified information and is implemented in software and hardware throughout the world to encrypt sensitive data

AES-256 – (Advanced Encryption Standard) is a specification for the encryption of electronic data established by the U.S. National Institute of Standards and Technology (NIST) in 2001.

AgCommand – AGCO's telemetry tool and one of the key enabling technologies powering its Fuse Connected Services

ARIMA – Autoregressive Integrated Moving Average

ARMA – Autoregressive Models: Provide a simple but effective form of dynamic machine-learning algorithm; when a value from a time series is regressed on previous values from that same time series

ARRA – The American Recovery and Reinvestment Act of 2009; an economic stimulus package enacted by the 111th United States Congress and signed into law by President Barack Obama on February 17, 2009

Assisted Services – Rather than making and implementing the decisions to improve the security, availability, performance and change, you offer advice and let the owner of the product manage the changes

AWS – Amazon Web Services

BARG – The pressure, in units of bars, above or below atmospheric pressure

Boot – When the machine powers up and is the first software to run

Brake cylinder PSI – The amount of pressure applied to brake cylinders

Brake pipe airflow – A flow meter provides air mass flow rate into the brake pipe

Brake pipe PSI – The current PSI of the brake pipe

CAV – Constant Air Volume: supply a constant airflow at a variable temperature — vary the airflow at a constant temperature

CBC – Complete Blood Count

CCU – Consolidated Controller Unit: monitors and controls the movement of the shearing arms to accuracies of two inches

CISC – Complex Instruction Set Computing

Classification – The prediction problem if the outputs are discrete values (predictive model is known as a classifier)

Cluster – A collection of input data vectors that is similar according to some metric

Clustering – A set of techniques for discovering patterns or "clusters" within input data

CMU – Communications Management Unit

Code Blue – Used to indicate a patient requiring resuscitation or in need of immediate medical attention, most often as the result of respiratory or cardiac arrest

Combine harvester – Also simply called a *combine*; a machine that harvests grain crops

CPU – Central Processing Unit

CRISP cycle – Based around exploration, it iterates on approaches and strategy rather than on software designs

CRM – Customer Relationship Management

CTF – Controlled Traffic Farming: A management tool used to reduce the damage to soils caused by heavy or repeated agricultural machinery passes on the land

DMZ – Demilitarized Zones: May be used to protect the process control system from the Internet and the business network

Dongle – Plugs into the OBD-II diagnostic port and collects data on how many miles are driven, what times of day a vehicle is in operation and how hard a driver brakes

DSL – Digital Subscriber Line

Dynamic machine learning – Concerned with the analysis of sequence or temporal data for which the standard independence assumptions inherent in many machine-learning algorithms do not apply

EDA – Exploratory Data Analysis: Initial steps of a machine-learning project

EHR – Electronic Health Record

Electrical impedance – Traditional method for counting cells; whole blood is passed between two electrodes through an aperture so narrow that only one cell can pass through at a time

EMR – Electronic Medical Record

Encryption – The process of encoding messages or information in such a way that only authorized parties can read it

Endothermic process – describes a process or reaction in which the system absorbs energy from its surroundings; usually, but not always, in the form of heat.

Epic Inserter – Device that can stuff envelopes at a rate of 22,000 pieces per hour while also allowing quick changeovers to different envelope types

Equalizing reservoir PSI – A small reservoir used on locomotives to regulate the brake pipe

ERP – Enterprise Resource Planning

ESP – Event Stream Processing

ETL – Extraction, Transformation and Loading: The process of extracting data from source systems and bringing it into a data warehouse

Event detection – Detect if something happens

Event identification – Identify what happened

Event quantification – Diagnose event

Eventual consistency – Database changes are eventually propagated to all nodes (typically within milliseconds) so queries for data might not return updated data immediately

Feature engineering – Task of determining a suitable representation of the raw input data that maximizes the performance of a machine-learning model

Feature vector – Resulting data vector used as the input to the model

FEMP – Federal Energy Management Program of the U.S. Department of Energy

Fertilizer Spreader – Spreads fertilizer; rate of flow is calibrated for each product (e.g., grain), while sensors measure the opening of the aperture, spreading width is entered into the onboard computer, and forward speed is taken from GPS

Firewall – A network security system that monitors and controls the incoming and outgoing network traffic based on predetermined security rules

Fixed-size vector – A number of input-data values

Fluorescent flow cytometry – Used to analyze physiological and chemical properties of cells; it can also be used to analyze other biological particles in urinalysis analyzers

FMEA – Failure mode and effects analysis, also "failure modes," plural, in many publications, was one of the first highly structured, systematic techniques for failure analysis.

FRA – Federal Railroad Administration

GAI – Green Area Index

GDSP – Global Data Services Platform

Global SIM – Provides a single means (SKU) for products to be distributed worldwide.

GPRS – General Packet Radio Service; a data service on 2G or 3G cellular networks

GPS – Global Positioning System

Ground trothing – Scanning and confirming

GUI – Graphical User Interface: A tool used to help formulate queries

Gyroscope – A spinning wheel or disc in which the axis of rotation is free to assume any orientation by itself; a sensor that can provide orientation information but with greater precision

Hardening – Having all good software and no bad software

HDFS – Hadoop Distributed File System: A Java-based file system that provides scalable and reliable data storage designed to span large clusters of commodity servers

Health monitoring or condition monitoring – Tasked with building an algorithm that can predict if an engine is operating normally or, alternatively, operating in a novel or abnormal way that may indicate a problem within the engine

Historians – Time-series databases

HMI – Human-Machine Interface

HR – Human Resources

HSPA – High Speed Packet Access

HVAC – Heating, Ventilating and Air Conditioning

Hydronic surface heater (aka: a ground heater) – Designed to warm soil during a concrete pour in the winter

IAS – Intelligent Agricultural Solutions

IDE – Integrated Development Environment: Software that provides comprehensive facilities to computer programmers for software development

IoP – Internet of People

IoT– Internet of Things

ISDN – Integrated Services for Digital Network

JACE – Java Application Control Engine: A series of embedded computer hardware devices that act in an area-controller capacity to distribute real-time control functions across an Ethernet bus in a large system

JVM – Java Virtual Machine

KPIs – Derived sensors (e.g., daily production rate)

Labeled dataset – An input/output pair consisting of the input vector together with the desired output value (label)

LAI – Leaf Area Index

Laser flow cytometry – A laser-based, biophysical technology employed in cell counting, cell sorting, biomarker detection and protein, by suspending cells in a stream of fluid and passing them by an electronic detection apparatus; more expensive than impedance analysis, due to the requirement for expensive reagents, but returns detailed information about the structure of blood cells

LEADER – A fuel-saving application that decreases the cost of maintenance by reducing coupler fatigue, wheel wear and brake shoe wear. It also dramatically increases throughput, particularly when integrated with a dispatch planner

Line-of-sight range – From antenna A you can see antenna B

LNG – Liquefied Natural Gas

LOCOCOMM – A CMU applicable to both GE and non-GE locomotives

Longwall mining – A form of underground coal mining where a long wall of coal is mined in a single slice (typically 0.6–1.0m thick). The longwall panel (the block of coal that is being mined) is typically 3–4km long and 250–400m wide

Longwall shearer – A relatively small component to the entire longwall-miling system controlled by complex algorithms onboard the machine

Longwall system – A mining system composed of the shearer, powered-roof-support system, armored face conveyor, belt conveyor, power supply, monorail and pump stations

LPWAN – Low Power Wide Area Network: Designed for wireless, battery powered Things

Machine data – The state of the blood analyzer or the gene sequencer

Magnetometer – Measurement instrument used for two general purposes: to measure the magnetization of a magnetic material like a ferromagnet, or to measure the strength and, in some cases, the direction of the magnetic field at a point in space

Mapping – Takes the form of a mathematical function, which is governed by a set of parameters (or weights)

MapReduce – A programming model and an associated implementation for processing and generating large data sets with a parallel, distributed algorithm on a cluster

Middleware – The software that connects software components or enterprise applications. The software layer that lies between the operating system and the applications on each side of a distributed computer network. Typically, it supports complex, distributed business software applications.

ML – Machine Learning

MM SCFH – Flow measured in cubic meter per hour

MQTT – (formally MQ Telemetry Transport) is an ISO standard (ISO/IEC PRF 20922) publish-subscribe-based "lightweight" messaging protocol for use on top of the TCP/IP protocol.

NDVI – Normalized Difference Vegetation Index

Nomic data – Data that describes what the machine is measuring, such as properties of soil or blood

Normality model – Test new input data against this model and evaluate the probability that the data is indicative of the system operating normally (i.e. that the input data could have been *generated* by the normality model with high probability)

NoSQL – Originally referring to "non SQL" or "non relational" database; provides a mechanism for storage and retrieval of data that is modeled in means other than the tabular relations used in relational databases

Novelty or Anomaly detection – The identification of new or unknown data that a machine learning system has not been trained with and was not previously aware of, with the help of either statistical or machine learning based approaches

O&M – Operations and Maintenance

OEMs – Original equipment manufacturers

OLAP – Online Analytical Processing: Performs multidimensional analysis of business data and provides the capability for complex calculations, trend analysis and sophisticated data modeling

One-factor authentication – A process for securing access to a given system, such as a network or website, that identifies the party requesting access through only one category of credentials

OPC / OLE for Process Control – A software interface standard that allows Windows programs to communicate with industrial hardware devices; OPC is implemented in server/client pairs. The

OPC server is a software program that converts the hardware communication protocol used by a PLC into the OPC protocol

OS – Operating System

OSI – Open Systems Interconnection: Conceptual model that characterizes and standardizes the communication functions of a telecommunication or computing system, without regard to their underlying internal structure and technology

OSISoft's PI system – One of the earliest time-series databases

Output values – Estimating one or more desired quantities of interest

Packaging – A major discipline within the field of electronic engineering that includes a wide variety of technologies

Patch – A Piece of software designed to update a computer's software

PDC – Phasor Data Collector

Pedometer – A sensor used to count the number of steps the user has taken

PII – Personally Identifiable Information

PLC – Programmable Logic Controller

PMU – Phasor Measurement Unit: Takes measurements at the power-frequency voltage, current and phasor angle (i.e. where you are on the power sine wave)

Predictive model – Provides a mapping from the input-data vector to the desired output value(s)

Prescription maps – Maps created by farmers by uploading soil-type data, historical-yield data and aerial imagery into farm management software

Product-as-a-Service – Manufacturer retains ownership and takes full responsibility for the security, availability, performance and change of the product in return for a recurring charge

PSIG – Pounds per Square Inch Pauge

PTC – Positive Train Control

Quad C – NYAB's packaging of the National Instruments CompactRIO with a QNX system

Query – A specific request for a subset of data or for statistics about data, formulated in a technical language and posted to a database system

RDBM – Relational Database Management System

Reaping – The cutting of the grain stalks

Regression – The prediction problem if the outputs are continuous values (predictive model is known as regression model)

REST – **Representational state transfer** or **RESTful** web services are one way of providing interoperability between computer systems on the Internet.

RISC – Reduced-Instruction Set Computer

RTOS – A real-time operating system; an operating system intended to serve time-critical applications

SaaS – Software-as-a-Service

SAE J1939 – The bus standard used for communication and diagnostics among vehicle components

SAM Car - Semi-autonomous motorcar

SCADA network – A system for remote monitoring and control that operates with coded signals over communication channels (using typically one communication channel per remote station)

Seal 1 Differential Pressure – The pressure between seal supply and compressor suction; the key control parameter to maintain the seal pressure as higher than the natural gas pressure inside the case

Segregate machine data – Data that describes the state of the machine such as its operating temperature and battery level

Service and Support – Product sales bundled with warranty or service contracts

SHA-256 – The **SHA** (Secure Hash Algorithm) is one of a number of cryptographic hash functions. A cryptographic hash is like a signature for a text or a data file.

SiP – System-in-a-Package; alternative to SoC

SKU – A single means for products to be distributed worldwide

SLA – Service Level Agreement

SoC – System-on-a-Chip; one of the packaging technologies used in high volume

SPL – Search Processing Language

SQL – Structured Query Language: A special-purpose programming language

Supervised learning – A predictive model that maps an input pattern to a desired output value

Synchrophasor – The resulting measurement of synchronized real-time measurements of multiple remote measurement points on the grid

Tag – A data point for each input sensor

Threshing – The separating of grain from the stalks

TLS – Transport Layer Security: Cryptographic protocols designed to provide communications security over a network; frequently referred to as 'SSL'

Two-pipe approach – Describes both machine information and *nomic* information. For example, a gene sequencer may have sensor information describing the reagent or voltage level of the machine (machine information) but also deliver genomic information — your DNA sequence.

UDP broadcast/multicast protocol – Further increases the volume of network traffic

UHF – Cellular option capable of 1–12 miles, depending on the terrain

Unsupervised learning – The finding of clusters in a set of input data that does not require any output values to be present in the dataset

VAV – Johnson Controls' Variable Air Volume; provides airflow, discharge air temperature, damper position and heat output readings continuously, which are logged in 15-minute intervals

VoIP – Voice over IP

VPN – Virtual Private Network

WBC – White Blood Cell Count

Winnowing – When wheat is tossed into the air to separate it from the chaff

Workflow or process management – Software used to orchestrate a step-by-step sequence of actions

Index of Vendors

7-Eleven 92
9REN 68

A

AGCO xv, 8, 29, 41, 108, 119, 121, 159-60, 162-4, 166-7, 213
Advantech 244
Air Force Research Laboratory 234
Allen-Bradley 52
Amazon xvii, 7, 41, 62, 67, 93
Amazon Web Services (AWS) 67, 242
Amtel 21
Appareo 29, 41
Apple 21-22, 235
Arduino 21, 23
ARM 11, 19, 22
Arrayent 40, 59
Arrow Electronics 244-245, 247-248
AspenTech 58, 143, 198
AT&T 133, 227
August Farms xv, 100, 106, 213-14, 217
Autodesk Fusion Connect xv, 14, 236, 238-239
Aviation 235
Ayla Networks 40

B

Ball Aerospace & Technologies Corp 234

Freescale Semiconductor 234

Index of Terms

A

abnormal engine behavior   76-7
accelerometer   5, 20-1, 34, 112, 241
ACID properties   57
ACM (AGCO Connectivity Module)   29, 162, 241
AGCO service   163
AgCommand   218, 242
agricultural machines   ix, 8, 28, 100, 167, 213
air-as-a-service   105
American Recovery and Reinvestment Act (ARRA)   204, 242
analyzers, hematology   29-30
antenna   xiii, 37, 39-40, 45, 249
aperture   30, 216, 244, 246
application layer   ix, xiii, 40-1, 120
applications
  low-data-rate   46, 187
  service-management   107-8
  time-critical   23, 253

B

C

K

Kaeser   66

L

M

McCrometer water sensors 38
measurements, discharge pressure sensor 198
mesh network of intermediate devices 46, 187
middleware x, 12, 16, 92-3, 103, 106, 113, 208, 250
mining equipment 139, 146
mining equipment-as-a-service 147
model prediction 199, 201
moisture 218-19
multi-year service agreements 13

N

N-Min tests 220
NASDAQ 180
natural gas 99, 174, 193
network security 42
nomic data x, 53, 97, 108, 146, 213, 237, 250
normalized difference vegetation index (NDVI) 219, 250
NoSQL x, 11, 55, 57-8, 60, 65, 250
novelty detection x, 76, 78

O

oil x, 33, 50, 52, 65, 83, 94, 103, 122, 145, 193-4, 196, 198, 201-2, 219
oil pressure sensor 162
On-line Analytical Processing (OLAP) 74, 251
OPC 51, 196, 198, 251
Open Systems Interconnection (OSI) 35, 251
OS, real-time 23

P

Packaged IoP Applications xi, 107
Packet Radio Service 246
patches 24, 46, 62, 69, 114, 186-8, 252
PDC (Phasor Data Collector) 205-8, 252
pediatric cardiology 238
pedometer 21, 252
per square inch gauge (PSIG) 195, 252

RPM Sensor   162
RTOS (real-time operating system)   23, 141, 153, 253
RTUs   227-8
run-time environments   22-3

S

SAS Enterprise Miner   207-8
satellite   x, 37, 49, 133-4
SD cards   219-20
Search Processing Language (SPL)   61, 173, 254
security   ix, 4, 6, 11, 24, 31, 42-3, 62, 67, 93, 95-6, 108, 113, 126,
   237-8
security appliances   52
security features   113
Security for IoT applications   108
security patches   93, 114
security services   92, 127
Sensium   188
sensor data   32, 132-3, 144-5, 152, 195, 199
  historic   87, 190
sensors   5, 11, 19-21, 27-9, 31-4, 66, 112-13, 124-5, 132-3, 151-2,
   170-1, 179, 196, 198-201, 219-20
  agronomic   218-19
  conductivity   162
  decreasing cost of   xviii, 7
  soil-moisture   226
  utility grid power   6
SensorState   152
servers   4, 22, 47, 53, 126, 163, 173, 180, 229
Service and Support Contracts   96
service contracts   13, 95-6, 104, 124, 129, 167, 234, 254
  classic   147
service economy   xii, 236
service industries   105
service interruptions   211
Service Level Agreement   124, 254
service level agreement (SLA)   124, 254
service machines   122
service plans   155

services
  better 8, 93, 183
  cloud-based 16
  direct rail 101
  higher quality 33, 127, 174, 237
  quality of x, 62, 93, 101, 174, 182
  storage cloud 62, 114
  wastewater treatment 66
shearer 99, 141-2, 145, 249
Similarity analysis xiv, 209-10
SiP (system-in-package) 25, 254
software
  bad 24, 42, 114, 247
  good 24, 114, 247
software-as-a-service 6, 147, 253
software industry 12, 91, 95, 147
software platform 32
software upgrades 48, 153
soil 28, 98, 160, 214, 219, 221, 226, 230, 244
soil temperature 226
Specialized applications 66, 92
SPL (Search Processing Language) 61, 173, 254
sprayers, liquid xiv, 214, 217, 220
spreader 28, 98, 215-16
SQL (Structured Query Language) 55-8, 74, 121, 254
SQL databases, connection service provider's 180
SQL engineers 236
SQL RDBMS x, 56, 58
SSL (Secure Sockets Layer) 47, 126, 255
stack, device-independent software 13, 126
Stuxnet 24
substations 204, 207
surface mining 139
surface water 223-4
system-in-package (SiP) 25, 254

T

technologists 114, 119
TLS (Transport Layer Security) 47, 126, 255

Topcon X30   214-17, 220
tractors   140, 159, 166-7, 215, 220
tractors-as-a-service   167
train control systems   31, 84, 131
train operator   101, 120, 135
training   73, 76-7
training simulators   31, 131, 134
trains   xviii, 32, 49, 73, 76, 85, 98, 101, 131-7

U

Ultra-High Frequency (UHF)   38, 227, 255
utilities   8, 99, 103, 105, 119, 177, 236

V

Variable Air Volume (VAV)   171, 255
VPN connection   133, 207

W

WBC (white blood cell)   29, 255
Weather Station   xiv, 225-6, 230
white blood cell (WBC)   29, 255
WiFi   ix, 37-8, 46-9, 107, 120, 133-4, 179, 187, 217
wind turbines   ix, xviii, 5, 8, 27-8, 58, 70, 94, 104, 112, 234, 239
winnowing   28-9, 160, 218, 255
wireless   45, 48, 186, 249

Y

Z

ZigBee   ix, 37, 45-6, 48, 107, 120, 187-8